Rooted in the Chants of Slaves, Blacks in the Humanities, 1985–1997

Recent Titles in
Bibliographies and Indexes in Afro-American and African Studies

Health of Black Americans from Post Reconstruction to Integration, 1871–1960: An Annotated Bibliography of Contemporary Sources
Mitchell F. Rice and Woodrow Jones, Jr., compilers

Blacks in Film and Television: A Pan-African Bibliography of Films, Filmmakers, and Performers
John Gray, compiler

Daddy Grace: An Annotated Bibliography
Lenwood G. Davis, compiler

African Studies Thesaurus: Subject Headings for Library Users
Freda E. Otchere

Chester Himes: An Annotated Primary and Secondary Bibliography
Michel Fabre, Robert E. Skinner, and Lester Sullivan, compilers

A Bibliographical Guide to African-American Women Writers
Casper LeRoy Jordan, compiler

Invisible Wings: An Annotated Bibliography on Blacks in Aviation, 1916–1993
Betty Kaplan Gubert, compiler

The French Critical Reception of African-American Literature: From the Beginnings to 1970, An Annotated Bibliography
Michel Fabre, compiler, with the assistance of Rosa Bobia, Christina Davis, Charles Edwards O'Neill, and Jack Salzman

Zora Neale Hurston: An Annotated Bibliography and Reference Guide
Rose Parkman Davis, compiler

Roots of Afrocentric Thought: A Reference Guide to *Negro Digest/Black World*, 1961–1976
Clovis E. Semmes, compiler

African American Criminologists, 1970–1996: An Annotated Bibliography
Lee E. Ross, compiler

Contemporary African American Female Playwrights: An Annotated Bibliography
Dana A. Williams

Rooted in the Chants of Slaves, Blacks in the Humanities, 1985–1997

A Selected Annotated Bibliography

Compiled by
Donald Franklin Joyce

Bibliographies and Indexes in Afro-American and African Studies,
Number 38

GREENWOOD PRESS
Westport, Connecticut • London

Library of Congress Cataloging-in-Publication Data

Joyce, Donald F.
    Rooted in the chants of slaves, Blacks in the humanities,
  1985–1997 : a selected annotated bibliography / compiled by Donald
  Franklin Joyce.
      p. cm.—(Bibliographies and indexes in Afro-American and
  African studies, ISSN 0742–6925 ; no. 38)
  Includes bibliographical references and index.
  ISBN 0–313–30477–7 (alk. paper)
    1. Afro-Americans—Bibliography. 2. Humanities—United States—
  Bibliography. I. Title. II. Series.
  Z1361.N39J694   1999
  [E185]
  016.973′0496073—dc21   99–11305

British Library Cataloguing in Publication Data is available.

Library of Congress Catalog Card Number: 99–11305
ISBN: 0–313–30477–7
ISSN: 0742–6925

First published in 1999

Greenwood Press, 88 Post Road West, Westport, CT 06881
An imprint of Greenwood Publishing Group, Inc.
www.greenwood.com

Printed in the United States of America

The paper used in this book complies with the
Permanent Paper Standard issued by the National
Information Standards Organization (Z39.48–1984).

10 9 8 7 6 5 4 3 2 1

TO

LEON FORREST
1937–1997

A FRIEND

AND

A WRITER'S WRITER

Contents

Acknowledgements

Without the assistance of many people, this work would not have become a reality. I am grateful to many librarians and their assistants in interlibrary loan departments across the United States who provided the sources cited in this bibliography. At Austin Peay State University, Carol Kimmel, the assistant in the Library Loan Unit of the Information Services Department, has my deepest gratitude for processing, without complaint, several hundred requests for sources I have used. Pamela Magrans, graduate assistant in the Languages and Literature Department at the University, allowed me to use her fine sense of sentence syntax, spelling and diction in proofreading copy, "gratis," for which I am grateful. To Lucy Suiter, an assistant in the University Library's Circulation/Reserves Department, I am immensely thankful for typing and retyping with great accuracy many sections of the work. And, finally, I extend my gratitude to Rosemary Stevenson, Afro-American Bibliographer at the University of Illinois-Urbana Library, for the exceptional index she has created for this work.

Introduction

Rooted in the Chants of Slaves, Blacks in the Humanities , 1985-1997: A Selected Annotated Bibliography, like its predecessor, *Blacks in the Humanities, 1750-1984* (Greenwood Press, 1986), presents annotated citations to published and unpublished sources in the humanities by and about Black Americans. However, unlike the former work, *Rooted in the Chants of Slaves* includes sources that appeared between 1985 and 1997.

Scope: General reference sources in the humanities and sources in ten humanistic disciplines are presented: philosophy, religion, library science, journalism, folklore, linguistics, visual arts, performing arts, music and literary criticism. Within each discipline except visual arts, sources in five literary formats are included: reference books; treatises and commentaries; biographical works; periodical articles; and dissertations. In visual arts, these five formats and catalogues of art exhibitions are represented.

Arrangement: Citations are numbered sequentially throughout the work. Within a discipline, sources are grouped under a literary format. An author, title, and specific subject index with reference to citation number provide access to the entire work.

General Reference Works: An Overview

BIBLIOGRAPHIES

001.   Davis, Nathaniel, comp. *Afro-American Reference: An Annotated Bibliography of Selected Sources.* Westport, CT: Greenwood Press, 1985.

   Citing 642 sources in African American history and culture which have reference value, this compilation has large sections on the humanities. Annotations for entries focus on the research potential of sources.

002.   Manat, G. P., comp. *Guide to Books on Black Americans.* New York: Nova Science Publishers, 1995.

   This one-volume bibliography lists 2,295 fiction and non-fiction titles on African American life and history published between 1990 and 1994. The entries are reproductions of main entry Library of Congress catalog cards arranged alphabetically by author or title. A subject index, listing many subjects in the humanities, contains references to entry number.

003.   Southern, Eileen and Josephine Wright. *African-American Traditions in Song, Sermon, Tale and Dance, 1600s-1920: An Annotated Bibliography of Literature. Collections, and Artworks.* New York: Greenwood Press, 1990.

   A comprehensive work, this extensively annotated bibliography provides a broad survey of primary materials on African American folk-arts from the 1630s to 1920. A total of 2,328 entries are included. A valuable bibliography of sources used to compile this work is presented. Specific name, subject and song-title indexes enhance access to this major reference work in African Americana.

INDEXES

004.   *The Kaiser Index to Black Sources, 1948-1986.* New York: Carlson Publishing Company, 1992.

Developed by the New York Public Library's Schomburg Center for Research in Black Culture, this massive five-volume work indexes more than 10 periodicals and newspapers published between 1948 and 1986. It contains 174,000 entries on every phase of Black life and history. Arranged alphabetically by Library of Congress subject headings, each entry includes the title of the article, title of the publication, date and page. Many subjects in the humanities are represented.

005.   Stevenson, Rosemary M., comp. *Index to Afro-American Reference Sources.* Westport, CT: Greenwood Press, 1988.

This unique source is an analytical index to over 150 reference sources on the Black experience. Arranged alphabetically under specific subjects, citations include: title of the article; title of the work in which the article is found; and inclusive page numbers. Many areas of the humanities are covered in this work.

ENCYCLOPEDIAS AND ALMANACS

006.   *The African American Almanac.* L. Mpho Mabunda, editor. Foreword by Chuck Stone. 7th edition. Detroit: Gale Research, Inc., 1997.

Formerly the *Negro Almanac, The African American Almanac* is a comprehensive ready-reference source with an abundance of factual, tabular and statistical information on all phases of African American life and culture. Titles of some of its twenty-seven chapters which are devoted to the humanities are "Media," "Blues and Jazz," "Popular Music," "Fine and Applied Art," "Classical Music," "Religion," "Performing Arts." An appendix lists African American recipients of selected national awards. A comprehensive bibliography on Africana and African Americans as well as specific subject indexes add to the reference value of this work.

007.   *The African American Encyclopedia.* Michael W. Williams, editor. New York: Marshall Cavendish, 1993, 6 v., Suppl., Kibibi Voloria Mack, editor, 1997, 1 v.

This well-researched multi-volume work presents current information on every area of African American life. Profusely illustrated, entries in this encyclopedia range from one paragraph to 5,000 words. Many subjects in the humanities such as the "Visual Arts," "Theater," and "Television" are treated in extensive articles with appendix bibliographies. The supplementary volume, released in 1997 contains 434 new articles and updated entries on 71 articles.

008.   *Encyclopedia of African-American Civil Rights: From Emancipation to Present.* Edited by Charles D. Lowery and John F. Marszalek. Westport, CT: Greenwood Press, 1992.

With entries arranged alphabetically by specific subjects, this one-volume work focuses on the Black American's struggle for civil rights in the United States from 1863 to the present. Many of the 800 entries contain information on Black involvement in the humanities in the United States such as "Journal of Negro History"; "Jubilee Singers"; "Rose McClendon Players"; and "New Negro

Movement." All entries are signed and have selected bibliographies.

009.   *Encyclopedia of African-American Culture and History.* Edited by Jack Salzman and
       Others. New York: Macmillan, 1996.

       This exceptional five-volume work has a host of entries on Black personalities who
       made contributions to the humanities as well as entries to Black publications in the
       humanities. Covering the history and culture of African Americans in North America
       and focusing on the United States, this comprehensive multi-volume work covers the
       years from 1619 to the late 1990s. Entries range from one paragraph to 30 pages.
       Several subjects documenting Black Americans in the humanities are discussed in
       depth.   For example, there is a 12-page article entitled "Literature," by Arnold
       Rampersad, biographer of Langston Hughes. Among some of the other contributors
       are noted historians John Hope Franklin; David Levering Lewis, the Pulitzer Prize-
       winning biographer of W. E. B. DuBois, and historian Eric Foner. Over 1,000 black-
       and-white photographs illustrate articles throughout the work. All entries are signed
       with bibliographies.

DIRECTORIES

010.   *The African American Yellow Pages.* Edited by Stanton F. Biddle. New York: Holt,
       1996.

       Arranged alphabetically under 50 headings, this directory lists more than 2,000
       African American agencies, associations, and organizations.   Entries contain
       pertinent information on each entity. Many entries are listed under headings relative
       to the humanities such as "Writing," "Poetry," and "Music."

011.   *Black Americans Information Directory, 1994-95.* Third edition. Wendy Van de
       Sande, Editor; Ned Burels, Associate Editor. Detroit: Gale Research, Inc., 1993.

       A comprehensive guide to approximately 5,300 Black organizations, agencies,
       institutions, programs and publications on Black American life and culture, this
       directory is arranged in 18 categories. The following categories are related to the
       humanities: "Religious Organizations," "Library Collections," "Museums and Other
       Cultural Organizations," "Historically Black Colleges and Universities," "Black
       Studies Programs," "Research Centers," "Publications," "Publishers," "Broadcast
       Media," and "Videos." Entries include the following items: name of the
       organization; address; telephone and fax numbers; Chief Executive Officer; and an
       annotation describing the agencies services or product.

BIOGRAPHICAL DICTIONARIES

012.   *Black Women in America: A Historical Encyclopedia.* Editor, Darlene Clark Hine.
       Associate Editors: Elsa Barkley Brown; Rosalyn Terborg-Penn. New York: Carlson
       Publishing, Inc., 1993.

       A total of 804 entries are presented in this work: 641 are biographies of women of national and local prominence; 163 are devoted to topics and organizations where women play important roles. Arranged alphabetically, all entries are signed and have bibliographies. A classified list of biographies is a helpful finding guide to biographees who have made contributions to the humanities.

013.   Hawkins, Walter L. *African American Biographies: Profiles of 558 Men and Women*. Jefferson, NC: McFarland, 1992.

_____. *African American Biographies, 2: Profiles of 332 Men and Women*. Jefferson, NC: McFarland, 1994.

Arranged alphabetically by surname, the biographees in this two-volume work: (1) were born in the United States or spent their childhood in this country; (2) played important roles in the development of African American children; and (3) were alive after 1968. Entries are detailed with dates, facts and statistics. Two indexes in Volume I provide access by occupation and geographical area. Indexes in Volume II refer to biographies in both volumes. In the occupational indexes, listings under "Communications" and "Entertainers" are very helpful in locating biographers in the humanities.

014.   *Notable Black American Woman*. Edited by Jessie Carney Smith. Detroit: Gale Research, Inc., 1992.

Notable Black American Woman, II. Edited by Jessie Carney Smith. Detroit: Gale Research, Inc., 1996.

The first volume of this biographical dictionary presents 500 signed biographies of outstanding African American women who were prominent from the mid-18th century to the 1990s. The second volume, published in 1996, presents 350 additional signed biographies of African American women of achievement covering roughly the same period. Both volumes have occupational, geographical and subject indexes. Indexes in the second volume refer to biographies in both volumes. Excellent source for locating famous as well as little-known African American women who have made contributions to the humanities.

015.   *Who's Who Among African Americans, 1996/97*. Foreword by Marvin L. Winas, Pastor, Perfecting Church. Shirley Phelps, Editor. 9th Edition. New York: Gale Research, Inc., 1996.

Short biographical sketches of over 20,000 Africans are listed in this work. Arranged alphabetically, entries include: personal data; education, career highlights, honors and awards and addresses of each biographer. Entries can also be accessed by geographical and occupational indexes.

In the Wake of Alain Locke: Blacks in Philosophy

DIRECTORY

016. Outlaw, Lucius T. Comp. *Africana Philosophy the International Database.* Haverford, PA: Department of Philosophy, Haverford College, 1995. (African, African-descended Philosophers in Higher Education).

This is a directory of philosophers of African descent teaching at American universities. Each entry lists: name of philosopher; academic rank; university association; city and state; areas of specialization in philosophy.

SELECTED WORKS BY BLACK PHILOSOPHERS ON GENERAL TOPICS IN PHILOSOPHY

017. Banner, William Augustus. *The Path of St. Augustine.* New York: Rowman and Littlefield, 1996.*

Former Chair of Howard University's Department of Philosophy William Augustus Banner discusses St. Augustine's ideas on moral aspiration in this engaging study. Banner focuses on such facets of St. Augustine's philosophy as "The Pursuit of Wisdom"; "Being, Truth, and Goodness"; "Justice and Culture"; and "Nature and Grace."

018. Hardimon, Michael O. *Hegel's Social Philosophy: The Project of Reconciliation.* New York: Cambridge University Press, 1994.

Hegel believed that his nineteenth-century contemporaries were alienated from modern social institutions. He sought through his social philosophy to reconcile them with these institutions. Hardimon presents in this study a systematic account of Hegel's social philosophy as a project of reconciliation which also has meaning for present-day cultural concerns.

019. Jalloh, Chernor Maarjou. *Fichte's Kant Interpretation and the Doctrine of Science.* Washington, DC: The Center for Advanced Research in Phenomenology and the University Press of America, 1988.

The historical and systematic relationship between Kant and Fichte is the subject of this study. Jalloh attempts to discuss Fichte's interpretation of Kant's "Grundlage der Gasammten" (The Foundation of the Doctrine of Science).

020.   McFarlane, Adrian. *A Grammar of Fear and Evil: A Husserlian-Wittgensteinian Hermeneutic*. New York: Lang, 1996.

The phenomenon of fear as the primary context for the problem of evil is examined in this study. Evil is seen as a religious interpretation of life's troubling experiences. Fear is the primary experience on which this interpretation is built.

021.   Simpson, Lorenzo C. *Technology, Time and the Conversations of Modernity*. New York: Routledge, 1995.

Contemporary society's attitudes toward time and technology are critically considered in this fascinating study. Simpson explores technology and time in the contexts of hermeneutics, critical theory, rationality and relativism, narrative theory, and postmodernism.

022.   Thomas, Lawrence. *Living Morally: A Psychology of Moral Character*. Philadelphia: Temple University Press, 1989.

Focusing on moral motivation, Thomas assumes that to be moral is to be altruistic. To develop this thesis, Thomas uses the writings of ancient and modern philosophers as well as contemporary psychologists and sociologists.

SELECTED WORKS BY BLACK PHILOSOPHERS ON RACE AND RACISM

023.   Gordon, Lewis R. *Bad Faith and Antiblack Racism*. Atlantic Highlands, NJ: Humanities Press, 1995.

In lucid prose this study critically examines Satre's views on antiblack racism as an act of "Bad Faith." Purdue University philosopher Lewis Gordon analyzes the subject of race at its ontological foundation. His analysis is divided into five chapters: "Bad Faith"; "Logic Racism, Racist Logic"; "Antiblack Racism"; "God in an Antiblack World"; and "Critical Encounters."

024.   Outlaw, Lucius. *On Race and Philosophy*. New York: Routledge Press, 1996.

Haverford College philosophy professor Lucius Outlaw argues for the need of an African-oriented philosophy. He builds a strong case for the need to understand the nature of race and the nature of philosophy.

025.   West, Cornel. *Keeping Faith: Philosophy and Race in America*. New York: Routledge, 1993.

In this collection of seventeen previously published essays, West using "prophetic criticism" explores the existential conditions of race in America. Examining problems related to culture, the Black intellectual, and Black political engagement, West wonders whether Blacks, especially the Black philosopher, can keep faith in

America.

026.   West, Cornel. *Race Matters*. Boston: Beacon Press, 1993.

A collection of eight essays published previously between 1991-93 interpreting various aspects of race in the United States. Notable among these essays are "Nihilism in Black America"; "Demystifying the New Black Conservatism"; and "On Black-Jewish Relations."

027.   Zack, Naomi. *Race and Mixed Race*. Philadelphia: Temple University Press,1993.

Zack, a philosopher teaching at the State University of New York City and the offspring of a mixed-raced union, explores the possibility of mixed-race identity in America. She argues that genetics has proven that there has never been a "pure race" and that Whites identify themselves as White because there has never been a non-White among their forebears.

SELECTED EDUCATION AIDS IN
PHILOSOPHY BY BLACK PHILOSOPHERS

028.   Appiah, Anthony. *Necessary Questions: An Introduction to Philosophy*. Englewood Cliffs, NJ: Prentice-Hall, 1989.

Written for the beginning student or laymen interested in philosophy, this lucid "textbook" discusses how several great philosophers have addressed major philosophical questions. Among some of the questions discussed are: (1) What is a mind? (2) What is the law of nature? and (3) What does moral judgement mean?

029.   Gordon, Lewis R. *Fanon and the Crisis of European Man:An Essay on Philosophy and the Human Sciences*. New York: Routledge, 1995.

This study is offered as an "engagement" with Franz Fanon. The totality and complexity of Fanon's thought are examined from six perspectives: politics; social science; ideology; mythmaking; philosophical anthropology; and general philosophy.

030.   Harris, Leonard, ed. *The Philosophy of Alain Locke, Harlem Renaissance and Beyond*. Philadelphia: Temple University Press, 1989.

This is an anthology of Locke's published and unpublished writings. Selected and edited by Harris, the "texts" are introduced with an analytical essay entitled "Rendering of the Text" and a perspective afterword titled, "Rendering of the Texts." A chronology of important events in Locke's life as well as extensive bibliography of works by and about Locke are included.

031.   Hord, Fred Lee (Mzee Lasana Okpara) and Jonathan Scott Lee. *I Am Because We Are: Readings in Black Philosophy*. Amherst: University of Massachusetts Press, 1995.

This collection of 35 writings by Black thinkers presents a historical overview of Black philosophy from 1500 B.C. Egypt, "The Declaration of Innocence" from

The Book of the Dead, to Leonard Harris's essay "Postmodernism and Utopia, an Unholy Alliance" (in *Racism, the City and the State*, ed. By Malcolm Cross and Michael Keith, London: Routledge, 1993, 31-43). Editors Hord and Lee provide an enlightening and analytical introductory essay on the tradition of Black philosophy.

032.   Washington, Johnny. *A Journey into the Philosophy of Alain Locke.* Westport, CT: Greenwood Press, 1994.

Authored by a biographer of Alain Locke, this volume authoritatively discusses Locke's philosophy as revealed through his works. "Part I: Ethnic Identity and Conflicts" focuses on racial and ethnic issues in history, anthropology, social psychology and sociology. "Part II: Value Relativism" focuses on Locke's views on the development of individual values.

SELECTED WORKS ON THE AFRICAN AND AFRICAN AMERICAN EXPERIENCE

033.   Boxill, Bernard R. *Blacks and Social Justice.* Revised ed. Lanham, MD: Rowman & Littlefield, 1992.

A conscious effort was begun during the Reagan Administration to dismantle color-conscious policies established to bring justice to the lives of African Americans. In this revised edition of this work, originally published in 1984, philosopher Bernard Boxill refutes charges leveled against these policies. He challenges the conservative views on racial justice of economist Thomas Sowell, sociologist William Julius Wilson, as well as those of Glenn Loury and Shelby Steele.

034.   Ezorsky, Gertrude. *Racism and Justice: The Case for Affirmative Action.* Ithaca, NY: Cornell University Press, 1991.

In the wake of efforts to dismantle Affirmative Action, which were begun in the 1990s, this study attempts to affirm and defend the rationale behind them. Institutional and overt racism and their remedies are analyzed and assessed.

035.   Flack, Harley E. and Edmund Pellegrino, eds. *African-American Perspectives on Biomedical Ethics.* Washington, DC: Georgetown University Press, 1992.

In this report on a conference on biomedical ethics, five Black philosophers were among the presenters who critically explored the conjuncture of African and African American cultural values on Anglo-Saxon biomedical ethics. Transcripts of papers presented by the following Black philosophers are included: William A. Banner; Kwasi Wiredu; Leonard Harris; Jorge Garcia; and Laurence Thomas.

036.   Smith, Theophus Harold. *Conjuring Culture: Biblical Formations of Black America.* New York: Oxford University Press, 1995.

In this highly creative study, philosopher Smith explores systematically the "conjurational spirituality" of Black Americans. Using the notion of conjure,

Smith attempts to explain and decipher events, themes, literature and other facets of Black American culture.

037.   Thomas, Laurence. *Vessels of Evil: American Slavery and the Holocaust.* Philadelphia: Temple University Press. 1993.

In this enlightening comparison of American slavery and the Holocaust, Thomas, who is son of Jewish and African American parents, presents a critique on common-sense morality. American slavery and the Holocaust are used as aids to understanding the status of Jews and Africans in the United States.

SELECTED WORKS ON WESTERN PHILOSOPHY

038.   Onyewuenyi, Innocent Chilaka. *The African Origin of Greek Philosophy: An Exercise in Afrocentrism.* Nsukka, Nigeria: University of Nigeria Press, 1993.

The accepted origins of philosophy in Western Civilization are challenged in this well-documented study. Citing Egyptian texts and examining the doctrines of the Egyptian Mystery System, Onyewuenyi attempts to show that the basis for Greek philosophy emanated from early Black-Egyptian civilization.

039.   Wiredu, Kwasi. *Cultural Universals and Particulars.* Bloomington: Indiana University Press, 1996.

Ghanaian-born philosopher Kwasi Wiredu, who teaches at the University of South Florida, challenges Western philosophers who shy from claims of universality. Wiredu believes that universals are compatible with cultural particulars and make possible intercultural communication.

SELECTED ARTICLES BY BLACK PHILOSOPHERS IN BOOKS AND JOURNALS

040.   Birt, Robert. "A Returning to the Source: The Philosophy of Alaine Locke," *Quest*, 4:2, 103-13, Dec. 1990.

Birt provides a critical, but brief, examination of Locke's achievements in philosophy. Locke's major contribution to the development of philosophy, according to Birt, was as a value theorist and as a theorist of value relativism and cultural pluralism.

041.   Davis, Angela. "Afro Images: Politics, Fashion and Nostalgia." *Critical Inquiry*, 21:1, 37-45, Autumn 1994.

Davis reminisces about the late 1960s and early 1970s, when photographs of Davis wearing an Afro were popular in the mass media. These visual images portrayed her as a Black militant and communist. Today, she laments, that the same photographs are regarded by many as fashion statements instead of images that document a significant historic era in American history.

042.   Gyeke, Kwame. "Technology and Culture in a Developing Country." (In *Philosophy and Technology*, edited by Roger Fellows. New York: Cambridge University Press, 1995), 121-141.

The development of science and technology in a traditional African culture is examined in this study. Ghana is used as the focus.

043.   Harris, Leonard. "'Believe It or Not' or the Ku Klux Klan and American Philosophy Exposed," *APA Proceeding and Addresses of the American Philosophical Association*, 68:5, 133-137, May 1995.

In this well-documented essay, a Purdue University philosophy professor assails the American philosophy profession for its seeming conspiratorial lack of opportunities afforded Black philosophers. For example, Harris points to only two Black philosophers who hold endowed chairs in philosophy in American universities. The work of Harvard-trained philosopher Alain Locke in critical relativism as a form of pragmatism is not included in any philosophy course at Harvard. Too few Black philosophers sit on doctoral committees in philosophy in American universities. Harris concludes his sweeping indictment of American philosophy with a stinging assessment.

> The jaundiced nepotism of persons controlling faculty positions, endowed chairs, and professorships is irrevelant, except as evidence of Klan predicted consequences; merit, virtuous character, and the triumph of scholastic explains it all.

044.   Martinez, Roy. "Pedagogy, Philosophy and African American Students." *Teaching Philosophy*, 17(4), 351-359, December 1994.

In this article, Martinez shares the pedagogy he used to increase exponentially the philosophy majors at the all-Black female Spelman College in Atlanta. Martinez asserts that you initiate the process with what is already familiar to students. "Then, by actually engaging them in a complex of questioning, explaining, elucidating, and illustrating, the students subsequently succeed in approximating the ideal of what is being taught."

045.   Mills, Charles. "Non-Cartesian Sums: Philosophy and the African American Experience," *Teaching Philosophy*, 17(3), 223-243, September 1994.

Mills argues that one feature of the experience of persons of African descent in the New World has been that they are categorized as racial sub-human persons. Their "sum," correspondingly, has been differentiated from the Cartesian "sum" in being an assertion of personhood against the intellectual universe of White supremacy. Using this concept as a basis, Mills outlines a course on African American philosophy.

046.   Piper, Adrian M.S. "Making Sense of Value Ethics," (Symposium on Elizabeth Anderson's *Value in Ethics and Economics*), *Ethics*, 106(3), 525-537, April 1996.

Piper was a panelist on a symposium on Elizabeth Anderson's book, *Value in Ethics and Economics* (Cambridge: Harvard University Press, 1993), which was held at the Pacific Division Conference of the American Philosophical Association in 1995. In "Making Sense of Value Ethics," Piper's paper which was presented at the symposium, she discussed Anderson's meta-ethical arguments in ways that she hoped would "streamline her treatment of the normative and pragmatic ones somewhat."

047.   Serequeberhan, Tsenay. "Eurocentrism: The Case of Immanuel Kant," *The Philosophical Forum*, 27:4, 333-356, Summer 1996.

Eurocentrism, Serequeberhan asserts, is grounded in the belief that European existence is qualitatively superior to other forms of existence. In this essay Serequeberhan critically analyzes the philosophy of Immanuel Kant in the light of Eurocentrism.

048.   Thomas, Laurence. "Becoming an Evil Society: The Self and Strangers," *Political Theory*, 24(2), 271-295, May 1996.

The self and its relationship to strangers are the focus of this essay. Thomas asserts that a person's own sense of self regulates his attitude towards others. A society that lacks basic trust engenders in the individual a distrust of strangers.

049.   Washington, Johnny. "An Outline of an Economic Ethics for Developing Countries," *Journal of Social Philosophy*, 25910, 110-115, Spring 1996.

Washington discusses in this essay economic ethics for developing countries. Asserting that economic ethics is axiological in outlook, Washington focuses on the economic and ethical factors involved in economic ethics for developing countries.

050.   West, Cornel. "The Million Man March," *Dissent*, 33:1, 97-101, Winter 1996.

The significance of the Million Man March, held in Washington, DC on March 5, 1995, is the focus of this essay. Although some observers have interpreted the March as a manifestation of African American rage, West views it as a united stand against African American suffering and a genuine call for social change.

051.   Williams, Preston N. "An Analysis of the Conception of Love and Its Influence on Justice in the Thought of Martin Luther King, Jr.," *The Journal of Religious Ethics*, 18(2), 15-31, Fall 1990.

Dr. Martin Luther King, Jr. used the model of love-justice created by Paul Tillich in developing his philosophy. In this essay Williams analyzes the love-justice relationship in King's philosophy.

SELECTED DISSERTATIONS

052.   Dixon, Bobby R. "Master-Slave Dialectic in the Writings of Ralph Ellison: Toward a Neo-Hegelian Synthesis." Ph.D. dissertation, Indiana University, 1990.

Using a neo-Hegelian approach, Dixon employs Hegel's master-slave model to explain Ralph Ellison's interpretation of Blacks in contemporary American society.

As revealed in Elllison's novel *The Invisible Man* and his essays, Blacks and Whites in America are seen as constituting a unity of which they are unaware. Realizing this unity, Dixon argues, might be the only means of saving them from self-destruction.

053.   Eze, Emmanuel Ckhukwudi.   "Rationality and the Debates about African Philosophy." Ph.D. dissertation, Fordham University, 1993.

Based on the traditions of African philosophy, Eze creates a model of a meta-physical and epistemological framework that is grounded outside of the objectivism-realism found in philosophy today. Eze's model is derived from *Ifa* tradition, but maintains dialogue with the Western traditions of realism.

054.   Moody-Adams, Michele Marcia. "Moral Philosophy Naturalized: Morality and Mitigated Scepticism in Hume." Ph.D. dissertation, Harvard University, 1986.

Moody-Adams considers Hume's efforts to treat moral philosophy as a branch of the science of human nature. Hume's *Treatises* and *Second Enquiry* are the focus of this investigation.

055.   Nnam, Michale Nkuzi.   "Anglo-American and Nigerian Jurisprudence: A Comparison and Contrast in Legal Reasoning and Concept of Law."   Ph.D. dissertation, De Paul University, 1985.

In this study Nnam compares Anglo-American and Nigerian jurisprudence. Although there are similarities, there are major differences. For example, the traditional Nigerial concept of law is inseparable from religion, ethics and morals. By contrast, in Anglo-American jurisprudence there is a sharp separation of law and morals.

In Search of Salvation: Blacks in Religion

SELECTED REFERENCE SOURCES

056. *African American Religion: Research Problems and Resources for the 1990s: Proceedings of the Symposium: May 26, 1990, Schomburg Center for Research in Black Culture.* New York: The Center, 1992.

These proceedings include papers presented by notable scholars in African American religion at a symposium sponsored by the Schomburg Center's Preservation of Black Religion Heritage Project. Papers were presented on topics related to: (1) research denominations; (2) sources and perspectives on local church history; (3) music in the African American religious tradition; and (4) regionalism in Black church studies.

057. Bible. English. Authorized. 1993. *The Original African Heritage Bible: King James Version.* With special annotations relative to the African/Edenic Perspective. Nashville: J.C. Winston Publishing Company, 1993.

According to publisher Dr. James Peeples, the objective of *The Original African Heritage Bible* is "to interpret the Bible as it relates specifically to persons of African descent and thereby to foster an appreciation of multiculturalism inherent in the Bible." Using the King James Version of the Bible as the basis text, each chapter is prefaced with a commentary discussing the presence of Africa and persons of African descent with a corresponding footnote explaining the significance of the relationship. Included in this work are several essays by biblical scholars, theologians, anthropologists and archeologists on the presence of African and persons of African descent in the Bible.

058. *Directory of African American Religious Bodies: A Compendium by the Howard University School of Religion.* 2nd ed. Wardell J. Payne, editor. Washington, DC: Howard University Press, 1995.

This comprehensive source discusses the growth and development of religious bodies among African Americans in the United States from the colonial period to the present. Included are: (1) substantial essays on Baptists, Methodists, Pentecostal and

Catholic denominations; (2) entries for African American religious organizations; (3) profiles of African religious educational institutions; and (4) a descriptive listing of African American religious research projects.

059. Dupree, Sherry Sherrod. *African American Holiness Pentecostal Movement: An Annotated Bibliography.* New York: Garland, 1996.

Covering the years from the 1880s to the present, this source is a comprehensive annotated bibliography on the African American Pentecostal Holiness Movement. Books, periodical and newspaper articles, dissertations, sound recordings, videotapes, pamphlets, WPA reports, FBI reports, and church documents are included. Arranged by chapters devoted to various aspects of the Movement, citations within each chapter contain pertinent bibliographic data, brief annotation, and the location for the item cited. A comprehensive index contains specific subject and name index to the entire work.

060. Dupree, Sherry Sherrod. *Biographical Dictionary of African American Holiness Pentecostals, 1880-1990.* Washington, DC: Middle Atlantic Regional Press, 1989.

Containing more than 1,000 biographical sketches of African Americans and white Americans who have made contributions to the African American Holiness Pentecostal Movement, this source is a significant addition to African American biographical religious literature.

061. *Encyclopedia of African American Religions.* Edited by Larry G. Murphy, J. Gordon Melton, and Gary L. Ward. New York: Garland, 1994.

With approximately 1,200 entries, including some 30 topical essays on African American religion and 80 biographical sketches on African American religious leaders from the last decades on the 18th century to the present, this source is a one-volume ready-reference work. In each entry additional related sources are listed for further research. An extensive index provides access by personal name, organization and specific subject.

062. Gray, John. *Ashe, Traditional Religion and Healing in Sub-Saharan African and the Diaspora: A Classified International Bibliography.* Westport, CT: Greenwood Press, 1989.

One of the most comprehensive bibliographies on Black religion in Africa and the countries where persons of African descent were dispersed, this source includes works that were published from 1760 to the present. Arranged by classified categories, entries within each category have location symbols where the item cited can be found.

063. *Winston's Original African Heritage Study Bible Encyclopedia Concordance.* Compiled by James Peeples. Nashville: James C. Winston, 1996.

This concordance defines words and phrases, interprets concepts, describes geographical locations, and presents biographies of persons cited in *The Original African Heritage Study Bible* (see 057). Entries are arranged alphabetically. Some entries are illustrated.

AFRICAN AMERICAN RELIGIOUS HISTORY

Selected Treatises and Commentaries

064.   Dvorak, Katherine L. *An African American Exodus: The Segregation of the Southern Churches*. Brooklyn, NY: Carlson Publishing Co. 1991.

In the antebellum South most African Americans, both slave and free, worshiped with white Americans in the same church. Between 1861 and 1871, however, African Americans left white churches in the South and formed their own churches. Why? This study explores the exodus of African Americans from white southern churches after the Civil War.

065.   Jacobs, Claude F. and Kaslow, Andrew J. *The Spiritual Churches of New Orleans: Origins, Beliefs, and Rituals of African American Religion.* Knoxville: University of Tennessee Press, 1991.

Using a variety of ethnohistorical techniques, two anthropologists conducted this study on Black spiritual churches in New Orleans. It focuses on church histories, beliefs, and rituals.

066.   Lincoln, C. Eric and Mamiya, Lawrence. *The Black Church in the African American Experience.* Durham: Duke University Press, 1990.

Using sociological theory and methodology, this comprehensive study of the Black church examines the history and practices of the major Black Protestant denominations. Extensively researched, this source includes over 40 skillfully designed statistical tables illustrating selective characteristics of the Black church.

067.   Raboteau, Albert J. *A Fire in the Bones: Reflections on African American Religious History.* Boston: Beacon Press, 1995.

In this collection of essays an African American historian interprets the significance of key events and personages in the religious history of African Americans. Among the essays included are "African American Exodus and American Israel;" "How Far the Promised Land?" "Black Religion and Black Protest;" and "Richard Allen and the African American Church Movement."

068.   Smith, Edward. *Climbing Jacob's Ladder: The Rise of Black Churches in Eastern Cities, 1740-1877.* Washington, DC: Smithsonian Institution Press, 1988.

As a result of the Great Awakening of 1740, many African Americans, slave and free, were converted to Christianity and joined white churches. After experiencing discrimination in many white churches, African Americans left these churches and began establishing their own churches. The Protestant churches founded by African Americans between 1740 and 1877 in the eastern cities of the United States are the focus of this history. Profusely illustrated with reproductions of rare documents, daguerreotypes and photographs, this work presents the history of each church as well as profiles of major and minor African American church leaders of the period.

069.   Taylor, Clarence. *The Black Churches of Brooklyn.* New York: Columbia University Press, 1994.

Several ministers associated with the Black churches of Brooklyn, New York have achieved national prominence as civil rights advocated such as Garner C. Taylor, Willliam A. Johns, Herbert Daughtry and Al Sharpton. In this history Taylor traces the history of the Black churches of Brooklyn from the mid-nineteenth century to the present focusing on the roles their ministers and congregations have played in forging the social, economic, spiritual, political and cultural life of African Americans.

Black Preaching and Sermonizing

070.   Crawford, Evans. *The Hum & Response in African Preaching,* by Evans Crawford with Thomas Troeger. Nashville: Abingdon, 1995.

African American folk preaching is analyzed by the Acting Dean of Howard University's School of Religion. This analysis focuses on such preaching techniques as call/response, musicality, sermon pause "hum thought."

071.   Davis, Gerald L. *I Got the Word in Me and I Can Sing It, You Know: A Study of the Performed African American Sermon.* Philadelphia: University of Pennsylvania Press, 1985.

Sermons of three African American preachers, dissimilar in personality, are analyzed using the emic (phonemic) and the etic (phonetic) approaches. In his analysis, Davis describes the character and function of the elements used in the preaching styles employed by each preacher.

072.   Hubbard, Dolan. *The Sermon and the African American Literary Imagination.* Columbia, MO: University of Missouri Press, 1994.

The sermon is one of the many rituals of the Black church which has influenced the development of African American literature. In this unique literary study, Dolan Hubbard, discusses the use of sermons in the works of Ralph Ellison, James Baldwin, Zora Neale Hurston, James Weldon Johnson, Frances Ellen Watkins and Frederick Douglass.

073.   Mitchell, Henry H. and Thomas, Emil M. *Preaching for Black Esteem.* Nashville: Abingdon, 1994.

How are sermons developed to enhance Black self-esteem? Henry Mitchell and Emil Thomas, two distinguished Black preachers, discuss historical, cultural, and theological examples of Black esteem and present written transcripts of sermons illustrative of Black self-esteem which they delivered to their congregation.

074.   Pipes, William H. *Say Amen Brother! Old-Time Negro Preaching: A Study in American Frustration.* Detroit: Wayne State university Press, 1992.

"Old-time" African American preaching had its origins among slaves in the 1730s and developed uninterrupted until the early 1830s when all meetings among slaves, including religious services where preaching occurred, were stopped by slave owners in reaction to the Nat Turner Slave Revolt of 1832. Since that time variation of "old-time" preaching have survived in some southern rural African American communities like Macon County, Georgia. This work, originally published in 1951 and released in a revised edition in 1992, is a classic study based on six sermons, examples of "old-time" preaching, which were recorded in Macon County, Georgia. With insightful brilliance, Pipes analyzes the transcripts of the sermons commenting on the content, organization and delivery style of each sermon.

075.   Waters, Kenneth L., Sr. *Afro-Centric Sermons: The Beauty of Blackness in the Bible.* Valley Forge, PA: Judson Press, 1992.

Ten sermons by the reverend Kenneth L. Waters, Sr. expounding the African World View are presented in this collection. They were selected by Waters because: "They embrace all the Afro-centric themes that I have tried to address."

BLACK MINISTRY

076.   McNeil, Jesse Jai, Sr. *The Preacher-Prophet in Mass Society.* With epilogue by Samuel DeWitt Proctor. Edited by Amos Jones, Jr. Nashville: Townsend Press, 1994.

First published in 1961, this collection of classic lectures by an outstanding National Baptist minister/scholar offers rare and insightful advice to ministers in urban communities. McNeil, who pastored at Detroit's Tabernacle Baptist Church for many years, challenges urban minister to: understand the urban social landscape; communicate effectively with the urban masses; re-evaluate their "call" to preach; adopt forceful speaking skills; and develop sermons which are faithful to the central themes of the Bible.

077.   Myers, William H. *God's Yes Was Louder Than My No: Rethinking the African American Call to Ministry.* Grand Rapids, MI: W. B. Erdmans; Trenton, NJ: Africa World Press, 1994.

The "call to ministry" stories told by several African American ministers are the subject of this unique study. The narratives of the ministers are discussed and analyzed in the light of six stages of the "call to ministry" experience: (1) early religious exposure; (2) call experience; (3) struggle; (4) search; (5) sanction; and (6) surrender.

078.   Myers, William H. *The Irresistible Urge to Preach: A Collection of African American "Call" Stories.* Atlanta, GA: Aaron Press, 1992.

A collection of the transcripts of eighty-six "call to ministry" stories by African American ministers. These stories were recorded in interviews conducted between 1985 and 1991. Ministers from eight denominations are included. One-fourth of the ministers are women. Ministers from three generations and every geographical area of the United States is represented. This collection is a companion volume to the author's *God's Yes Was Louder Than My No: Rethinking the African American Call to Ministry.* (see 077)

079.   Roberts, J. Deotis. *The Prophethood of Black Believers: An African American Political Theology for Ministry.* Louisville: Westminister John Knox Press, 1994.

Ecumenical in vision, this study addresses various aspects of ministry in the Black church. Among some of the topics discussed are: "Ministry in the Black Tradition"; "Black Women in the Ministry"; "The Black Minister and Politics"; "The Music Ministry in Black Churches."

080.   Rooks, Charles S. *Revolution in Zion: Reshaping African American Ministry, 1960-1974: A Biography in the First Person.* New York: Pilgrim Press, 1990.

The Fund for Theological Education (FTE) was founded in 1954 to recruit talented college students for the ministry in Protestant churches. One component of the FTE's program was the recruitment and training of Blacks for pastorates in Black Protestant churches. Between 1960 and 1974, Charles Rooks was prominently associated with this component of the program. In this biographical narrative, Rooks discusses the impact that Black recruits have had on the reshaping of African American ministry in the United States.

081.   Washington, Joseph R. *Rulers of Reality & the Ruled Race: The Struggle of Black Ministers to Bring Afro-Americans to the Full Citizenship in America.* Lewiston, NY: E. Mellen, 1990.

The role African American ministers have played throughout the history of organized religion in America to gain for African Americans equal rights is the focus of this study. Among some of the African American ministers whose activities are profiled are Richard Allen, Lemuel Haynes and Alexander Crummell.

082.   Wheeler, Edward L. *Uplifting the Race: The Black Minister in the New South, 1865-1902.* Lanham, MD: University Press of America, 1986.

In the intervening years from the end of the Civil War to 1902, the Black church became a major force in improving the lives of African Americans in the South. This study considers the pivotal role of Black church ministers in uplifting the Black community in the South. It focuses on: (1) the Black minister as part of the Black community; (2) the theology of uplift practiced by Black ministers; (3) the politics of the Black ministerial elite; and (4) education and the ministerial elite.

Black Theology

083.   *African Roots: Towards an Afrocentric Christian Witness.* Edited by Michael I.N. Dash, L. Rita Dixon, Darius L. Swann, Ndugu T. Ofari-Atta.   Lithonia, GA: SCP/Third World Literature and Publishing House, 1994.

Conceived at the Pan-African Christian Church Conference (PACCC), which was held in Atlanta in July 1988, this volume is a collection of writings by some of the participants who focused on the African origins of Christianity. Among some of the essays in the collection are: "The Bible and the African Experience," by Charles B. Copher; "Ancient Africa and the Old Testament," by Randall Bailey, and "The Ethiopian Church and Its Living Heritage," by Archbishop Yesehao of the Ethiopian Orthodox Church.

084.   Bascio, Patrick. *The Failure of White Theology: A Black Theological Perspective.* New York: Peter Lang, 1994.

White theology, Bascio asserts, has failed Black people. In this insightful treatise, the author offers reasons for the development of Black theology, discusses the contributions of Black theology to white and Black communities, and discourses on the difference and similarities of Black theology and classical theology.

085.   *Black Theology: A Documentary History.* Edited by James H. Cone and Gayraud S. Wilmore.   2nd rev. ed.   Maryknoll, NY: Orbis Books, 1993.

This two volume history is a collection of primary documents that trace the thematic development of Black theology from 1966 to 1992. Volume One covers the years 1966 to 1979; Volume Two is devoted to the years 1980 to 1992.

086.   Cone, James H. *A Black Theology of Liberation.* Twentieth Anniversary Edition. Maryknoll, NY: Orbis Books, 1990.

Originally published in 1970, this treatise outlines a systematic theology which empowered Black people spiritually to liberate themselves from oppression: an oppression which white theology has sanctioned. This edition presents critical commentaries by Gayraud Wilmore, Robert McAfee Brown, Pablo Richard, Rosemary Radford Ruether, K. C. Abraham and Delores S. Wilson.

087.   Evans, Anthony. *Are Blacks Spiritually Inferior to Whites?*   Wenonoh, NJ: Renaissance Productions, 1992.

One of the most devastating myths perpetuated throughout American history has been the concept of the spiritual inferiority of Black people, Evans asserts. In this commentary Evans presents evidence from Black religious history and Black theology to refute the myth of the spiritual inferiority of Black people.

088.   Hopkins, Dwight N. *Shoes That Fit Our Feet: Sources for Constructive Black Theology.* Maryknoll, NY: Orbis Books, 1993.

Five sources in the African American tradition for developing a Black theology are discussed in this work. They are: (1) slave narratives, spirituals and autobiographies; (2) fictional works by African American authors like Toni Morrison; (3) characters in African American folklore such as: "Brer' Rabbit," "Shine' and "The Trickster;" (4) the political/religious ideas of W.E.B. DuBois; and (5) the religious philosophies of Malcolm X and Dr. Martin Luther King, Jr.

089.   Salley, Columbus and Behm, Ronald. *Whdt Color Is Your God? Black Conscious and the Christian Faith.* New York: (Citadel Press) Coral Publishing Group, 1995.

This treatise seeks to explain how Christianity, as perceived and practiced by the "status quo," has historically oppressed Blacks. The authors suggests to white Christians some positive measures to make Christianity a force that meets the objective and subjective needs of the Black community.

090.   Stewart, Carlyle F. *Street Corner Theology: Indigenous Reflections on the Reality of God in the African American Experience.* Nashville: Winston-Derek, 1990.

Street-corner theology's primary resources are down-home grassroots traditions that shaped and influenced the Black experience in America. This work profiles the lives of extraordinary African Americans who have been nurtured by this indigenous African American cultural theology, a form of Black theology.

Denominations

Baptist

091.   Fitts, Leroy. *A History of Black Baptists.* Nashville: Broadman Press, 1985.

This history of Black Baptist documents the activities of early independent churches beginning in the late eighteenth century, the regional and state associations which sprung into existence between the 1840s and 1880s, and the national organizations that began in 1895 with the National Baptist convention USA. Chapters are devoted to: (1) the exodus of Black Baptists from white Baptist churches in the South; (2) Black Baptists and missions; (3) Black Baptists involved in education, and (4) Black Baptists in the socio/political arena.

092.   Harvey, William J. *Bridges of Faith Across the Seas.* Philadelphia: The Foreign Missions Board of the National Baptist Convention, USA, Inc., 1989.

Black Baptist missionary work abroad was begun when George Lisle organized churched in Jamaica in 1783 and was continued when Lott Carey established churches in Africa in 1821. This work by William J. Harvey, the Executive Secretary of the Foreign Missions Board of the National Baptist Convention. USA, Inc., is an authoritative and well-documented history of Black Baptist foreign missionary activities from 1783 to the 1980s.

093.   Pitts, Walter F. *Old Ship of Zion: The Afro-Baptist Ritual of African Dispora.* New York: Oxford University Press, 1993.

The rituals as they are used in Afro-Baptist churches in sermons, musical performances and body gestures are described and analyzed by Walter F. Pitts, a linguist, anthropologist and ethnomusicoligist. The study is based on field work which Pitts conducted in several rural Texas Afro-Baptist churches.

094.   Washington, James Melvin. *Frustrated Fellowship: The Black Baptist Quest for Social Power.* Macon, GA: Mercer University Press, 1986.

Since the establishment of independent Black Baptist churches in the 1780s, Black Baptists have been a major force in the development of the Baptist faith in the United States. Black Baptists in their drive for freedom for all Black Americans have not always been supported by white Baptists. This study focuses on the history of the relationship between Black and white Baptists and the quest for freedom for Black Americans.

Catholic

095.   Davis, Cyprian. *The History of Black Catholics in the United States.* New York: Crossroads, 1995.

This is a comprehensive history of the Black Catholic community in the United States. After discussing the roots of Black Catholicism in ancient Africa, Davis traces the development of Catholicism in the United States from the mid-1700s to the present.

096.   McDonogh, Gary W. *Black and Catholic in Savannah, Georgia.* Knoxville: University of Tennessee Press, 1993.

A southern white anthropologist studies the growth and development of Black Catholicism in Savannah, Georgia. Using the research methods of an anthropologist, McDonogh presents: (1) an ethnohistory of religion in Savannah's Black community; (2) a history of the Catholic church in the city's Black community; and (3) an analytical description of the structure and leadership of Catholicism in the city's Black community today.

097.   Ochs, Stephen. *Desegregating the Altar: The Josephites and the Struggle for Black Priests, 1871-1960.* Baton Rouge: Louisiana State University Press, 1990.

The St. Joseph Society of the Sacred Heart (The Josephites) has been devoted to evangelizing among African Americans. This study documents the Josephites relentless struggle to train African American priests in the face of institutional and regional-laymen racism from the last decade of the nineteenth century through 1960.

The Church of God and the Saints in Christ

098.   Wynia, Elly M. *The Church of God and Saints of Christ: The Rise of the Black Jews.* New York: Garland, 1996.

William Sanders Crowdy founded The Church of God and Saints of Christ in 1896 in Lawrence, Kansas. With a theology which is synthesis of Jewish and Christian elements, this denomination has grown to 213 churches throughout the United States, the West Indies and South Africa. This is a history of the church from 1896 to the present.

Lutheran

099.   Johnson, Jeff G. *Black Christians: The Untold Lutheran Story.* St. Louis, MO: Concordia Publishing House, 1991.

There are 132,000 Black Lutherans in the United States today. Authored by a retired Black Lutheran minister, this study documents the growth of Black Lutherans in the United States since the mid-1700s; examines the development of Black Lutheranism in the larger social context; and identifies strategies that Lutherans have used in working with Blacks in the New World.

Mormon

100.   Embry, Jessie L. *Black Saints in a White Church: Contemporary African American Mormons.* Salt Lake City, UT: Signature Books, Inc., 1995.

In 1978 the Mormon Church lifted restrictions on its African American members. Black men could be ordained to the Latter Days Saints priesthood. Black men and women could be married in Mormon temples and receive "temple endowment" ordinance. Consequently, African American membership, since 1978, has grown into the thousands. This study, based on the Latter Days Saints (LDS) African American Oral History Project interviews of 224 African American Mormons, is a group biography of African Americans in the Mormon Church.

Muslim

101.   Barboza, Steven. *American Jihad: Islam After Malcolm X.* New York: Doubleday, 1994.

More than 50 African American Muslims discuss the impact of Malcolm X on their religious beliefs and experiences through transcribed interviews and autobiographical essays. Some of the famous personalities included in this volume along with lesser-known Muslims are Muhammad Ali and Kareem Abdul-Jabbar.

102.   McCloud, Aminah Beverly. *African American Islam.* New York: Routledge, 1995.

Written by an Islamic scholar, this highly readable study provides an excellent historical and contemporary overview of African American Islam. Seventeen Islamic communities are described: the early communities which existed between 1900 and 1960; and the contemporary communities from 1960 to the present. Chapters are devoted to: (1) family structure and other aspects of domestic life; (2) the tensions between Darul Islam and Darul Harb; and (3) women in Islam.

Unitarian

103.   Morrison-Reed, Mark.   *Black Pioneers in a' White Denomination.*   With an introduction by Andrew Young. Boston: Unitarian Universalist Assn., 1994.

Ethelred Brown, who established the Harlem Unitarian Church in New York City in 1920, and Lewis A. McGee, who helped found the interracial Free Religious Fellowship in Chicago in 1947, were Black pioneers in the Unitarian Universalist Association of North America. Mark Morrison-Reed, a Black Unitarian minister, chronicles the activities of these two Black pioneering ministers and discussed the significance of Black presence in Unitarian Universalism.

SELECTED BIOGRAPHICAL WORKS

104.   Dean, David M. *Defender of the Race: James Theodore Holly, Black Nationalist Bishop.* Boston: Lambeth Press, 1995.

Born in Washington, DC in 1829 to free parents, James Theodore Holly became the first Black bishop in the Episcopal Church when he was consecrated Bishop of Haiti in 1861. This is the first book-length biography of this nineteenth century pioneering Black cleric, emigrationist and missionary.

105.   Jemison, Theodore J., Sr. *The T. J. Jemison, Sr. Story.* Nashville: Townsend Press, Sunday School Publishing, National Baptist Convention USA, 1994.

From 1982 to 1994, T. J. Jemison was president of the National Baptist Convention, USA, inc., the largest Black religion denomination in the United States. Born in Selma, Alabama in 1919, Jemison was the son of a Baptist minister who served as the Convention's president from 1943 to 1953, D.V. Jemison. In this autobiography, Jemison shares his experiences as a Baptist minister, but also describes with rare insight the workings of the National Baptist Convention, USA, Inc.

106.   Klein, Michael. *The Man Behind the Sound-Bite: The Real Story of Reverend Al Sharpton.* New York: Castillo International, 1991.

Reverend Al Sharpton, "The Sound-Bite," is one of the most charismatic, social activist Black ministers in the public eye today. This biography chronicles Rev. Sharpton's life from his boyhood days in the 1950s to the demonstration at Bensonhurst on January 2, 1991, when he was stabbed by a protester.

107.   Oldfield, J.R. *Alexander Crummell, 1819-1898 and the Creation of an African American Church in Liberia.* Lewiston, NY: Mellen, 1990.

Alexander Crummell was one of the leading African American intellectual and religious personalities in the nineteenth century.   An Episcopal minister and proponent of Black emigration to Liberia, Crummell attempted to establish the National Church of Liberia. This biographical study focuses on Crummell's involvement in the aborted founding of this church.

108.   Seraile, William. *Voice of Dissent: Theophilus Gould Stewart.* New York: Carlson, 1991.

Theophilus Gould Stewart was a leader in the African Methodist Episcopal Church in the second half of the nineteenth century. He pastored several prominent AME churches in major cities, served as Chaplain of the Twenty-fifth U.S. Colored Infantry, and was president of Wilberforce University. This biography documents and discusses Stewart's philosophy and the major events in his prolific career.

109.   Thomas, Herman E. *James W.C. Pennington: African American Churchman and Abolitionist.* New York: Garland, 1995.

In antebellum America, James W.C. Pennington was a fiery minister and social reformer based in the free northern African American community. This biography chronicles his life, highlighting his activities as a minister and a Black abolitionist.

PERIODICAL ARTICLES

110.   "Black megachurches," *The Christian Century,* July 3, 1996, vol. 113, no.21, p.686.

Throughout the United States several African American churches have evolved into "Megachurches" to serve the spiritual needs of. affluent middle-class African Americans. The growth and complex organization of a few of these churches are described and discussed in this article.

111.   Depriest, Tomika and Jones, Joyce. "Economic Deliverance Through the Church," *Black Enterprise*, 27:7; 1950200, February 1997.

Many Black inner-city churches have developed successful economic programs which are enriching the Black community. Successful programs at four Black inner-city churches are described in this article. The churches are: Northwest Baptist Church, Houston, TX; Wheat Street Baptist Church, Atlanta, GA; Allen AME Church of Queens, New York, NY; and First AME Church, Los Angeles, CA.

112.   Hunt, Larry L. "Black Catholicism and Secular Status: Integration, Conversion and Consolidation," *Social Science Quarterly*, 77:4; 842-860, December 1996.

This study explores the relationship between Catholic religious affiliation and the socio-economic status of African Americans. Some of the findings revealed that: (1) African American Catholics are more likely to attend racially integrated churches that other African Americans; and (2) in the north, African American Catholics have a higher socio-economic status than other African Americans.

113.   Jennings, Willie James. "Wrestling with a Wounding Word: Reading the Disjointed Lives of African American Spirituality," *Modern Theology*, 13:1; 139-171, January 1997.

African Americans have always wrestled with the duality of Christian theology. It has had a life-sustaining effect as well as a wounding effect on African American spirituality. In this article, Jennings explores three arguments involving the effects of Christian theology on African American spirituality.

114.   Maxwell, Joe. "Building the Church (of God in Christ)," *Christianity Today*, 40:4; 22-28, April 8, 1996.

Founded by Charles Harrison Mason, the Church of God in Christ is today the fifth largest and one of the fastest growing religious denominations in the United States. Maxwell presents a brief profile of Mason, describes a typical church service and discussed the growth of the denomination and its current leadership.

115.   Nelson, Timothy J. "Sacrifice of Praise: Emotion and Collective Participation in an African American Worship Service," *Sociology of Religion*, 57:4; 379-380, Winter 1996.

Based on structured interviews and participant observation, this study focuses on the "emotional" worship service in an African American Episcopal (AME) church in a lower socioeconomic neighborhood in Charleston, South Carolina. Nelson discussed reasons for the continued vitality of "emotional" worship services and attempts to explain the relationship between "emotionalism" and social class.

116.   Paris, Peter J. "The Ethics of African American Religious Scholarship," *Journal of the American Academy of Religion*, 64:3; 483-498, Fall 1996.

In this transcription of Peter J. Paris' presidential address before the American Academy of Religion, he observes that one of the results of equal educational opportunities for African Americans has been the development of African American religious scholarship. Lauding the efforts of the Academy in encouraging African American religious scholars, Paris notes that the emergence of Black theology in the 1970s was a major contribution to African American religious scholarship.

117.   Taylor, Robert Joseph, Linda M. Chatters, Rukmalie Jayakody and Jeffery S. Levin. "Black and White Differences in Religious Participation: A Multi-Sample Comparison," *The Journal for the Scientific Study of Religion*, 35:4; 403-411, December 1996.

DISSERTATIONS

118.   Campbell, Gilbert G., Jr. "Preaching from the Gospel of Mark As a Basis for Addressing Economic and Social Justice Issues in the African American Community." Ph.D. dissertation, United Theological Seminary, 1993.

The project described in this study was based on the Gospel of St. Mark. Sermons, using the Gospel of St. Mark, were preached to the congregation of The New Calvary Baptist Church in Norfolk, VA. The intent was to develop ministries in the congregation to confront five economic and social problems which plagued the local Black community. These problems were AIDS, homelessness, crack, poor health, delinquent and criminal youth.

119.   Collins, Annette Beverly. "African-American Pentecostalism As an Ecstatic Movement." Ph.D. dissertation, University of Chicago, 1996.

Using the tools of the "Religionwissenschaft School," a set of principles developed by nineteenth century German theologians to study religions scientifically, Collins analyzes African-American Pentecostalism. It concludes that the African American Pentecostalism is an ecstatic movement because of the distinct way it approaches, comprehends, knows and experiences the Sacred by repetition of the acts which happened at the original Pentecost.

120.   D'Apolito, Rosemary Ann. "An Analysis of the African American Catholic Congregation As a Social Movement. Ph.D. dissertation, Kent State University, 1994.

In 1989 Archibishop G. Augustus Stalling established The African American Catholic Congregation (AACC) in Washington, DC to address the problems facing African Americans. In this study D'Apolito seeks to determine whether AACC is a social movement responding to racism in the American Catholic Church and the American society.

121.   Ferguson, George Saint Anthony, Sr. "Stewardship and Discipline Development in the African American Church." Ph.D. dissertation, United Theological Seminary, 1994.

Enhancing stewardship and discipleship in the Christ Creative Baptist Church by employing a holistic approach was the focus of this dissertation project. The methodology used included: (1) a pre-project survey; (2) preparing sermons and teaching aids; (3) hosting revivals and seminars; (4) hosting "game nights"; and (5) a post-project survey.

122.   Flake, Floyd Harold. "The Religious, Social, Political and Economic Development Ministry of Richard Allen: A Model for the Twenty-First Century African American Church." D.Min. dissertation, United Theological Seminary, 1995.

Richard Allen, first Bishop of the AME Church, was one of the most powerful Black American leaders during the first 30 years of the nineteenth century. As a religious leader, Allen championed Black American's economic, social and political uplift. In this study Allen's ministry is studied as a model for Black ministers today who endeavor to lift their devastated communities out of poverty, crime and drugs.

123.   Haney, Marsha Snulligan. "Encountering Religious Pluralism: The Challenge of Islam and the Protestant African American Churches." Ph.D. dissertation, Fuller Theological Seminary, School of World Missions, 1994.

Haney asserts that contemporary Protestant African American churches seem to be unaware that they are in a pluralistic religious society. Consequently, these churches are unable to meet the challenges of the growth of Islam in the Black community. This study recommends a missional model that might be used by Protestant African American churches to bear witness of the Incarnation of Christ within this religiously diverse society.

124.   LaRue, Cleophus J., Jr. "What Makes Black Preaching Distinctive? An Investigation Based on Selected African-American Sermons from 1865-1915 in Relation to the Hermeneutical Discussion of David Kelsey." Ph.D. dissertation, Princeton University, 1996.

The sermons of John Jasper, Alexander Crummell, Francis Grimke, Daniel Payne, and Elias Morris are analyzed in this study. In his analysis, LaRue uses the David Kelsey concept of scriptural interpretation.

125.   McDonald, Isaac Lee. "A Study of the Effects of College Education on the African American Expectations of Preachers and Their Preaching." Ph.D. dissertation, Lancaster Theological Seminary, 1996.

The objective of this study was to determine whether the expectations of preaching are changing in African American churches with the increasing educational level of laity. Questionnaires were sent to 152 students taking courses in religion at Hampton University, 72 lay persons and 12 ministers in churches of the Eastern Virginia Association of the Southern Conference of the United Churches of Christ.

126.   Muir, Fareed Z. "Islam in America: An African American Pilgrimage Toward Coherence." Ph.D. dissertation, Temple University, 1993.

The Nation of Islam integration into the worldwide Islamic community has evolved over a number of years. Muir traces this evolution focusing in the roles played by Elijah Muhammad, Malcolm X and Warith Deen Muhammad.

127.   Pinn, Anthony Bernard. *"I Wonder As I Wander: An Examination of the Problem of Evil in African American Religious Thought."* Ph.D. dissertation, Harvard University, 1994.

The objective of this study is to present a historical and theological examination of the problem of evil in African American religious thought. This is achieved by analyzing the "musical expressivity" and writings of prominent African American religious leaders.

The Legacy of Edward Christopher Williams: Blacks in Libraries and Librarianship

SELECTED REFERENCE SOURCES

Directories

128. *Membership Directory of the Black Caucus of the American Library Association.* 4th edition. Edited by George Grant. Winter Park, FL: Published for the Black Caucus by 4G Publishers, 1996.

Over 1,000 African American librarians and persons interested in African Americans in libraries are listed in this directory. Arranged alphabetically by surname, each entry includes: (1) name of listee; (2) title; (3) place of employment; (4) address; (5) telephone number; and (6) fax number. The work is enhanced with indexes by type of library and by state.

Conference Proceedings

129. *Culture Keepers: Enlightening and Empowering Our Communities.* Proceedings of the First National Conference of African American Librarians, September 4-6, 1992, Columbus, Ohio. Edited by Stanton F. Biddle and Members of the BCALA NCAAL Conference Proceedings Committee. Newark, NJ: Black Caucus of the American Library Association, 1993.

These proceedings of the first national conference of African American librarians include papers and presentations by many of the country's leading librarians on "cutting edge" topics in African American librarianship. In addition to transcripts of an array of enlightening individual presentations and panel discussions on various topics, this volume includes complete transcripts of seven major conference papers. They are "Diversity in A. R. L. Libraries," by Kriza Jennings; "The Black Librarian, Black Author, Black Publisher: Connection," by Barbara Clark Elam; "Electronic Multi-Cultural Archives," by John H. Whaley, Jr.; "In Our Own Voices: African-American Academic Librarians Speak," by Deborah A. Curry and Glendora Johnson-Cooper; "Educating the Black Librarian and Information Professional for Librarianship for Leadership in the 21st Century," by Mary F. Lenox; "The Black Mother

Goose: A Collective Biography of African American Children's Librarians," by Fannette H. Thomas; "The Ancient Kemetic Roots of Library and Information Science," by Itibari M. Zulu; and "Marketing the Inner City Library," by Vandella Brown.

130.   *Culture Keepers II: Unity Through Diversity.* Proceedings of the Second National Conference of African American Librarians, August 5-7, 1994, Milwaukee, Wisconsin. Sponsored by the Black Caucus of the American Library Association. Edited by Stanton F. Biddle and Members of the BCLA-NCAAL Conference Proceedings Committee. Newark, NJ: Black Caucus of the American Library Association, 1995.

The transcriptions of one hundred and one presentations which addressed twelve areas of diversity are included in these proceedings. The eleven areas are: (1) Diversity and the Information Superhighway; (2) Diversity in Library and Information Science Education; (3) Diversity in Public Library Services; (4) Diversity in Academic Library Services; (5) Diversity in Law Librarianship; (6) Diversity in Media in Library Services Programs; (7) Diversity of Library Service to Children and Young People; (8) Diversity in International Programs; (9) Library and Information Resources and Services in West Africa; (10) Diversity in Recruitment and Professional Development; (11) Diversity in Special Materials, Special Collections, and Collection Development; (12)Diversity - Authors and Publishing.

131.   *Educating Black Librarians.* Papers for the 50th Anniversary Celebration of the School of Library and Information Sciences, North Carolina Central University. Edited by Benjamin F. Speller. With a foreword by E. J. Josey. Jefferson, NC: McFarland, 1991.

Included in this volume are papers presented at a symposium held during the 50th year anniversary celebration of the School of Library and Information Sciences at North Carolina Central University and reprints of articles related to issues which were discussed. Among the issues and topics addressed in these papers and articles are (1) recruitment of Blacks and minorities into the library profession; (2) the role of the Black library and information professional; (3) the impact of technology on library education; and (4) Annette Lewis Phinazee and North Carolina Central University School of Library and Information Sciences.

Bibliographic Aids

132.   *The African-American Mosaic: A Library of Congress Resource Guide for the Study of Black History and Culture.* Edited by Debra Newman Ham. With contributions by Beverly Brannan, Dena J. Epstein, Ronald Grim, Ardie S. Myers, David L. Parker, Rosemary Fry Plakas and Brian Taves. Washington, D.C.: Library of Congress (For sale by the Supt. of Docs., U.S.G.P.O), 1993.

The Library of Congress is one of the richest depositories of African American materials in the world. It began collecting materials on African Americans just after the War of 1812, when the private library of Thomas Jefferson which included materials on slavery and abolition, was purchased. Over the years due to the provisions copyright law and donations of private papers of some leading African American personages and organizations as Booker T. Washington, Carter G. Woodson, and the National Urban League, African American materials in the Library of Congress have grown tremendously. *The African American Mosaic* is a researcher's guide to African American materials in the Library of Congress. It is divided into three sections: "Part One: African-American in the Antebellum Period"; "Part Two: Forever Free - Emancipation and Beyond"; and "Part Three: The Pursuit of Happiness." Within each section there are three chapters which are bibliographic essays devoted to the Library holdings on a specific subject. Throughout the work there are illustrations from the Library's visual holdings. An author, title, and subject index provides excellent access to the work.

133.   New York Public Library. *Bibliographic Guide to Black Studies, 1997.* Boston: G.K. Hall, 1997.

Published annually since 1988, this bibliography is a dictionary catalog to new titles in Black Studies acquired by the New York Public Library.

134.   New York Public Library. Schomburg Center for Research in Black Culture. *Index to the Schomburg Clipping File.* Alexandria, VA: Chadwyck-Healy, 1986.

Begun in 1924 by the famed librarian, Catherine Latimer, and maintained until 1974, the Schomburg Clipping File is a collection of clippings from Black and white newspapers and periodicals which span the years from 1850 to 1974. In 1985 The Schomburg Clipping File was put on microfiche and distributed commercially by Chadwyck-Healy Publishers. This print index makes the valuable source on microfiche accessible.

TREATISES, STUDIES AND COMMENTARIES

Black Librarianship as a Profession

135.   *The Black Librarian in America Revisited.* Edited with an introduction by E.J. Josey, Metuchen, NJ: Scarecrow Press, 1994.

Black librarians working in library education, academic libraries, public libraries and special libraries share their experiences and expertise in this enlightening volume of twenty-six essays. Among some of the essays included are "Black Library Educators in the 1900s: Characteristics and Accomplishments," by Carolyn O. Frost; "Reflections on Being a (Minority) Librarian in Our Time," by D. Alexander Boyd; "A Black Dean of an ARL Library," by James F. Williams; "The Black Information Specialist in the R. & D. Environment," by Ina A. Brown; "Reflections of a Former State Librarian," by Ella Gaines Yates; "Librarians, Archivists and Writers: A Personal Perspective," by Ann Allen Shockley.

136.   McPheeters, Annie L. *Library Service in Black and White: Some Personal Recollections, 1921-1980.* Metuchen, NJ: Scarecrow, 1988.

In this personal narrative, pioneering librarian Annie L. McPheeters reminisces about the history and development of public library service to African Americans in the Southeast between the years spanning from 1921 through 1980. She focuses on the growth of public library to African Americans in Greenville County, SC; Rome, GA; and Atlanta, GA.

Cataloging and Classification

137.   Brown, Lorene B. *Subject Headings for African-American Materials.* Englewood, CO: Libraries Unlimited, 1995.

This work cites over 5,000 subject headings on and related to the African American experience. Brown has utilized authoritative sources in African American history as well as the Library of Congress Subject Headings (LCSH) to create this list. It differs from the LCSH in two ways: (1) "African American" is used instead of Afro-American"; and (2) "Historically Black Colleges and Universities" is used in place of "African American Universities and Colleges." This work is also available on CD ROM.

138.   Clack, Doris Hargrett. *Authority Control: Principles, Applications, and Instructions.* Chicago: American Library Association, 1990.

Written by the late Doris Hargrett Clack, an African American librarian who had a distinguished career as a leader in authority control in cataloging, this work covers the theoretical as well as the practical aspects of authority control. It provides a sound theoretical base to insure a thorough understanding of the practice of authority control.

Young Adult and Children's Literature

139.   *African-American Voices in Young Adult Literature: Tradition, Translation, Transformation.* Edited by Karen Patricia Smith. Metuchen, NJ: Scarecrow Press, 1994.

The fourteen essays in this collection present various views on the validity of African American young adult literature by librarians, literary critics and writers. Among the subjects discussed are biography, poetry, periodical literature, the novel, feminist literature and African literature.

140.   Khorana, Meena. *Africa in Literature for Children and Young Adults: An Annotated Bibliography of English-Language Books.* Westport, CT: Greenwood Press, 1994.

This annotated bibliography of 700 titles with an additional 120 titles cited in annotations covers titles published between 1973 and 1994. Citations are grouped in five chapters representing different geographical regions in Africa and one chapter which includes general books. The five regions are North Africa, West Africa, East Africa, Central Africa, and Southern Africa. Within each chapter citations are arranged under the following genres: traditional literature; fiction; poetry; biography;

and information books. The work has three separate indexes: author, title, and illustrator.

141.   MacCann, Donnarae and Woodward, Georgia, ed. *The Black American in Books for Children*. 2nd ed. Metuchen, NJ: Scarecrow, 1985.

In this classic collection of essays by children's librarians, artists, and cultural historians several significant issues relative to the presentation of Black Americans in children's books are discussed.   Among some of the topics covered are authenticity of Black characters, the evaluation of Blacks in children's books, and authors of children's books about Blacks.

142.   Rollock, Barbara T. *Black Authors and Illustrators of Children's Books*. 2nd ed. New York: Garland, 1992.

This useful reference source by the former Coordinator of Children's Services at New York Public Library presents biographical profiles of more than 150 authors and illustrators of children's books about persons of African descent. Books and sources by and about each author or illustrator are listed with their profiles. Appendix I describes various awards for children's books about Blacks and cites awardees. Appendix II lists publishers series. Appendix III lists all publishers which have released children's books about Blacks.

Black Bibliophiles, Past and Present

143.   *Black Bibliophiles and Collectors: Preservers of Black History*. Edited by Elinor DesVerney Sinnette, W. Paul Coates, Thomas C. Battle. Washington, DC: Howard University Press, 1990.

The lives and collecting activities of many major Black book collectors, contemporary as well as deceased, are discussed in this volume by scholars, librarians, book dealers and collectors in fourteen essays and two commentaries. The essays and commentaries were originally presented at "Black Bibliophiles and Collectors Symposium," which was held at Howard University, November 29-30, 1983.

144.   *Catalogue of the Charles L. Blockson Afro-American Collection:* A unit of Temple University Libraries. Edited by Charles L. Blockson. Philadelphia: Temple University Press, 1990.

Representing a lifetime of collecting by Charles L. Blockson, this collection, which bears his name, became a unit of the Temple University Libraries in 1984. Blockson was appointed curator. The Charles L. Blockson Collection consists of more than 30,000 books and bound periodicals as well as 15,000 broadsides, pamphlets, sheet music and other items. The Catalogue is arranged by broad subject classes. Within each subject class entries for items are arranged alphabetically by title. Entries for each item are numbered consecutively throughout the work. Entries may be accessed through three indexes: subject, name and title.

145.   Sinnette, Elinor Des Varney. *Arthur Alfonso Schomburg: Black Bibliophile and Collector: A Biography.* Detroit: The New York Public Library and Wayne State University Press, 1989.

Arthur Alfonso Schomburg, whose private collection of books and artifacts on persons of African descent was bought by New York Public Library and became the nucleus for its Schomburg Center for Research in Black Culture, was one of the great Black bibliophiles in the first quarter of the twentieth century. This first book-length biography traces his life from his birth in 1874 to his death in 1938 focusing on the last 47 years of his life.

PERIODICAL ARTICLES

146.   Badar, Barbara. "Connections - A Story in Three Parts," *The Horn Book,* 73:91-8, January/February 1997.

The lives and writing careers of historian Carter G. Woodson and writer/librarian Arna Bontemps are chronicled in relation to their contributions to the development of Black literature for children. The significance of both men's publications and activities for children are discussed substantively.

147.   Church, Phyllis E. "Sassy As a Jaybird: Brer Rabbit in Children's Literature," *Journal of Youth Services in Libraries*, 4; 243-248, Spring 1991.

Joel Chandler Harris' Brer Rabbit tales have been a popular success for generations of children and adults. The character of Uncle Remus, however, has become an unacceptable stereotype for contemporary readers. Additionally, the dialect used in Uncle Remus tales has become a problem for those who have retold the tales. Church discussed how some authors, namely Virginia Hamilton, Julius Lester and Van Dyke Parks, have tried to resolve these problems in works which they have written.

148.   Curry, Deborah A. "Your Worries Ain't Like Mine: African American Librarians and the Pervasiveness of Racism, Prejudice and Discrimination in Academe," *The Reference Librarian* nos. 45-46; 299-311, 1994.

Racism, Curry observes, in higher education and academic libraries has an adverse influence on the behavior of Black and minority librarians. It affects the recruitment and retention of Black and minority librarians. Initiatives for improving the working environment in academic libraries for Black and minority librarians is discussed in this essay.

149.   Gravois, Jim M. "Comparing Libraries of Public Historically Black Colleges and Their Counterparts," *College and Research Libraries* 56: 519-30, November 1995.

In order to desegregate public historically Black colleges and universities (HBCUs), the federal courts have mandated that libraries at these institutions be upgraded. This preliminary survey compares the libraries at HBCUs with traditionally white public colleges and universities. The following six variables are used in the comparison: (1) volumes per student; (2) salary expenditures per student; (3) salary expenditures; (4) total library staff per hundred students; (5) professional Librarians per hundred students; and (6) professional librarians as a percentage of total library staff.

150. Joyce, Donald Franklin and Jenkins, Betty L. "'...Aiming to Publish Books within the Purchasing Power of a Poor People...': Black-Owned Book Publishing in the United States, 1817-1987," *Choice* 26: 6; 907-913, February 1989.

This bibliographical essay identifies little-known sources which shed light on the book publishing activities of Black Americans between 1817 and 1987. These published and unpublished sources provide information on six types of Black-owned book publishers: religious publishers; institutions which engaged in book publishing; cultural and professional organizations which published books; civil rights organizations that published books; college and university book publishers; and commercial book publishers.

151. Lee, Ernest and Russell, Joan C. "Faces in the Crowd: Black Films in the 1970s," *Library Journal*, 115; 39-42, May 15, 1990.

The 1970s, the compilers of the filmography declare, was the decade of the greatest proliferation of Black films. After critically commenting on the major films released during the decade, Lee and Russell present an annotated filmography of all commercial Black films released in the 1970s. The films are rated. Films which are highly recommended for library collections are designated with a (*).

152. Margolies, Beth Anne. "Bibliographic Essay on Three African American Artists: William H. Johnson, Romare Bearden, and Jacob Lawrence," *Art Documentation: Bulletin of the Art Libraries Society of North America*, 13: 1, 13-17, Spring 1994.

Aimed at the serious researcher in African American art, with an introduction to general sources on the subject located in the museums, libraries and galleries of Washington D. C. and New York City. Bibliographic works by and about William H. Johnson, Romare Bearden, and Jacob Lawrence and their location in the two cities are discussed in detail.

153. Martin, Robert Sidney and Shiflett, Orvin Lee. "Hampton, Fisk, and Atlanta: The Foundations, the American Library Association, and Library Education for Blacks, 1925-1941," *Libraries and Culture* 31: 299-325, Spring 1996.

In 1925 the American Library Association, the Carnegie Corporation of New York, the General Education Board and the Julius Rosenwald Fund joined together in an effort to establish a library education program for African Americans in the South. Between 1925 and 1941 three historically Black colleges and universities were seriously considered as sites for a library school: Hampton Institute, Fisk University and Atlanta University. Based on primary documents, this well-researched article seeks to answer many questions about the project. Why was Hampton Institute selected over Fisk University as the first site for the library school in 1925? What forces and personalities continued to agitate for Fisk as a site through the 1920s and 1930s? Why did the Hampton Library School close in 1939? And why was a new library school opened at Atlanta University in 1941?

154.   Moses, Sibyl E. "The Influence of Philanthropic Agencies on the Development of Monroe Work's *Bibliography of the Negro in Africa and America.*" *Libraries and Culture* 31: 326-41, Spring 1996.

Work's *Bibliography of the Negro in Africa And America*, when it was published in 1928, was the most comprehensive bibliographic work to appear on persons of African descent to date. Moses discusses the roles played by three philanthropic agencies in the development of the project which eventually became the final publication: the Carnegie Corporation of New York, the Laura Spelman Rockefeller Memorial and the Phelps-Stokes Fund.

155.   Pyne, Charlynn Spencer. "The Burgeoning 'Cause,' 1920-1939: An Essay on Carter G. Woodson," *Library of Congress Information Bulletin* 53: 41-9, February 7, 1994.

Pyne, a collections development librarian at the LC's National Library Service for the Blind, describes Woodson's collecting and research efforts in documenting Black history from 1920 to 1930. Encouraged by LC's Manuscripts Division Chief during those years, J. Franklin Jameson, Woodson was able with Jameson's support and influence to win support from several philanthropic agencies for the Association for Study of Negro Life and History, the Associated Publishers and other projects.

156.   Ransom, Charles G. "Bibliographies of Microforms Relating to African-Americans," *Microform Review* 23: 64-76, Spring 1994.

The result of searches conducted on the University of Michigan online catalog, these bibliographies lists approximately 250 items. Citing books, periodicals, unpublished sources, the material in the bibliography is grouped under the following headings: biographies, civil rights, Civil War, colonization, economics, employment, freedmen, history, Michigan, music, news, papers, periodicals, politics, race, Reconstruction, religion, riots, segregation, slavery, social conditions, theses. Although the bibliography includes acquisitions through December 1992, future updates are planned. This edition of the bibliography is available on the Internet and, on the University of Michigan's gopher.

157.   Tucker, John Mark. "Let the Circle Be Unbroken: The Struggle for Continuity in African-American Scholarship," *Libraries and Culture* 31: 645-55, Summer/Fall, 1996.

Scholarship produced by African American librarians between 1970 and 1994 is reviewed and analyzed in this substantive book review essay. After discussing notable scholarly works in librarianship published by African American librarians from 1970 to the late 1980s, Tucker reviews three major works which were published in the 1990's. They are *Black Bibliophiles and Collectors: Preservers of Black History,* Edited by Elinor Des Verney Sinnette, W. Paul Coates, and Thomas Battle

(1990); *Black Book Publishers in the United States: A History of the Presses,* by Donald Franklin Joyce (1991); and *The Black Librarian in America Revisited,* Edited by E. J. Josey (1994).

DISSERTATIONS

158.   Ball, Patricia Bernice Huff. "African American Male Library Administrators in Public and Academic Libraries: A Descriptive Study." Ph.D. dissertation, University of Pittsburgh, 1993.

The study seeks to provide information on the status of African American male librarians in public and academic libraries. Sixty-five African American male librarians were surveyed using a mail questionnaire. Sixty questionnaires or 92.3% were returned and fifty-five or 84.6% were used to compile data. Some characteristics of the African American male library administrators were: (1) most were born in the South; (2) came from middle-class to working class families; and (3) were graduates of Atlanta University School of Library Service. Other findings of the study reveal how these librarians perceived racism and the "old boy" network as influences on their professional lives.

159.   Gollop, Claudia Joyce. "Health Information-Seeking Behavior of Urban Older African American Women." Ph.D. dissertation, University of Pittsburgh, 1993.

Using a fifty-item interview schedule, Gollop conducted in-person interviews with forty-five African Americans in Pittsburg to find out ways they obtained health information. Most interviewees reported that they received health information from their physicians, friends, and the mass media. Although most interviewees stated they thought the public library was a likely place to get health information, only twenty-four percent of interviewees were regular users.

160.   Gunn, Arthur Clinton. "Early Training for Black Librarianship in the U.S.: A History of the Hampton Institute Library School and the Establishment of the Atlanta University School of Library Service." Ph.D. dissertation, University of Pittsburgh, 1986.

In 1925 the Hampton Institute Library School was opened, making it the first library for African Americans in the United States. During its fourteen-year history, 183 men and women completed the program at the Library School. When the Hampton Institute Library School closed in 1939, it was subsequently followed by the opening of the Atlanta University School of Library Service in 1941. This study describes the development of library education for African Americans in the South by documenting the history of the Hampton Institute Library School and the establishing of the Atlanta University School of Library Service.

161.   McCann, Donnarae E. "The White Supremacy Myth in Juvenile Books About Blacks, 1830-1900." Ph.D. dissertation, The University of Iowa, 1988.

The origin and perpetuation of the myth of white superiority in juvenile books published in the United States from 1830 to 1900 is the subject of this ground breaking study. McCann describes the interaction between adult culture and children's literature during this period. Political, biographical and literary history are examined as well as the history of the church, school, press and other institutions which influenced childrens' lives.

162.   Malone, Cheryl Knott. "Accommodating Access: 'Colored' Carnegie Libraries, 1905-1925." Ph.D. dissertation, The University of Texas at Austin, 1996.

Between 1905 and 1925 the public libraries in several cities in the South received funds from the Carnegie Corporation of New York to construct branch libraries for African Americans. Focusing on Louisville, Houston, Nashville and New York City's Harlem, this study analyzes the different motivational forces and meanings involved in developing public library service to African Americans in southern cities and compared to providing public library service to African Americans in a northern city like New York.

163.   Mills, Emma Joyce White. "An Examination of Procedures and Practices in the Selection of Black Materials for Children's Collections of Public Libraries in the United States." Ph.D. dissertation, The Florida State University, 1987.

The objective of this study is to identify and examine practices and procedures employed by public libraries in the United States to select and acquire materials about Blacks for children. A sample of 202 library employees in public libraries throughout the United States responded to a mail questionnaire to obtain information about these practices and procedures.

164.   Phillips, Kathryn Bednarzik. "A Comparative Content Analysis of Illustrated African American Children's Literature Published Between 1900-1962 and 1963-1992." Ph.D. dissertation, The University of Oklahoma, 1995.

In this study samples of illustrated African American children's literature were analyzed. The methodology used included qualitative content analysis, comparative content analysis, and Eisner's artistic approach. The study revealed that illustrated children's literature about African Americans published between 1900 and 1962 depicted negative images about Blacks. However, literature from the later period presented more authentic representation of Blacks.

Defenders of the Race: Blacks in Journalism

SELECTED REFERENCE WORKS

Bibliographies

165. Hill, George H., et al. *African American Television Experience.* Los Angeles: Daystar Publishing Co., 1987.

   This source is the first book-length bibliography designed for the researcher/student to appear on Blacks in television. It is divided into fourteen broad classifications. Within each classification citations to books, chapters in books, journal articles, dissertations and theses are arranged alphabetically by author. Published and unpublished works which appeared from the late 1940s to the mid-1980s are included.

166. Hill, George H., *Black Radio in Los Angeles, Chicago, New York.* Carson, CA: Daystar Publishing Co., 1987.

   Focusing on Black radio in the Los Angeles, Chicago and New York City markets, this bibliography covers Black radio broadcasting from the late 1920s to the mid 1980s. Among its 786 entries there are citations to books, dissertations, journal articles, and radio station publications.

167. Hill, George, et al., *Black Women in Television: An Illustrated History and Bibliography.* New York: Garland Publishing Co., 1990.

   Spotlighting Black women in television, this source presents a brief illustrated history of Black women in the industry as actresses, directors, and news reporters. A bibliography of 703 citations to books, journal articles, dissertations and theses covers the involvement of Black women in television from the late 1930s to the late 1980s. The appendices list television awards won by Black women and television series where Black women had starring roles.

168.   Hill, George H. And Hill, Sylvia Saverson. *Blacks on Television: A Selectively Annotated Bibliography.* Metuchen, NJ: Scarecrow Press, 1985.

Editing books, journal and newspaper articles, dissertations and theses, this annotated bibliography includes sources which document Blacks' involvement in television from 1939 through the mid-1980s.

Guides

169.   Hill, George H. and Davenport, Robert P. *Shading "TV Guide" Black Side: A Book.* Los Angeles: Daystar Publishing Co., 1987.

TV Guide is a primary source for television information and programming. Over 800 articles which appeared about Black programming and Black entertainers in *TV Guide* between April 3, 1953 and May 7, 1987 are cited in this bibliography. Three indexes provide access to this work by subject/ author; programs; and video/film title.

170.   Potter, Vilma Raskin. *A Reference Guide to Afro-American Publications and Editors, 1827-1946.* Iowa City: Iowa State University Press, 1993.

After crtitquing several bibliographies on African American newspapers, Potter reproduces Warren Brown's *Checklist of Negro Newspapers in the United States, 1827-1946,* a pamphlet published in 1947 by the Lincoln University (MO) School of Journalism, which includes 467 newspapers. To access Browns' checklist Potter has created four indexes: (1) place-of-publication index; (2) year-of-publication index; (3) undated publication index; and (4) editors index.

Compilation

171.   *African American History in the Press, 1851-1899.* Detroit: Gale, 1996, 2 v.

Organized into chapters by year from 1851 to 1899, this is a compilation of more than 1200 newspaper news article, editorials and illustrations about African Americans from 13 major American newspapers and magazines for the years covered. This brilliantly conceived reference work has keyword, illustration and newspaper indexes.

Organizational Publication

172.   Dawkins, Wayne. *Black Journalists: The NABJ Story.* Expanded, updated, 2nd. edition. Merrillville, IN: August Press, 1977.

The National Association of Black Journalists (NABJ) was founded in 1975 by 44 Black journalists. Today its membership is over 1800 journalists. Dawkins describes the founding and history of this organization through 1995. Profiles of many of its members are included.

SELECTED COMMENTARIES AND TREATISES

Newspapers

173. Brown, Warren H. *The Social Impact of the Black Press.* New York: Carlton, 1994.

Since 1827 the Black press has existed in the United States. In this study Brown discusses how Black newspapers have addressed the social, economic, educational and political concerns of Black Americans since the birth of the Black press and the end of World War II.

174. Caldwell, Earl. *Black American Witness: Reports from the Front.* Editors: Lurma Rackey, Kenneth Walker. Washington, DC: Lion House Publishing Co., 1994.

For more than thirty years, Earl Caldwell has been one of America's most widely-read journalists. He has worked as a reporter for *The New York Herald Tribune, The New York Post,* and *The New York Times.* In the early 1970s, Caldwell began writing a column for *The Washington Star* and from 1979 to 1994 he was a columnist for *The New York Daily News.* This volume is a compilation of Earl Caldwell's columns which appeared three times a week in *The New York Daily News* between 1979 and 1994.

175. Hutton, Frankie. *The Early Black Press in America, 1827 to 1860s.* Westport, CT: Greenwood Press, 1992.

The secular Black press which operated in the free Black communities on the Northeast is the subject of this study. In Hutton's analysis of the Black press it is shown that not only was it concerned with antislavery, but substantively addressed women's rights, social morality, education of youth and other major issues of the period.

176. Kinshasa, Kwando M. *Emigration vs. Assimilation: The Debate in the African American Press, 1827-1861.* Jefferson, NC: McFarland, 1988.

Author Kinshasa has conducted a content analysis on Black Newspapers published between 1827 and 1861 to determine the views of editors and readers relative to emigration to Africa, the Caribbean, Central America, and assimilation. Over thirty-five Black newspapers were examined in this study.

177. Kobre, Sidney, et al. *A Gallery of Black Journalists Who Advanced Their Race....And Our Nation.* Hampton, VA: United Brothers and Sisters, 1993.

This history of the Black press is divided into three periods. They are: "Part I: The Pioneers: Pre-Civil War Era, 1827-1865;" "Part II: Black Journalism in the Gilded

Age, 1865-1900;" and "Part III: Black Journalism in the 20th Century, 1900-1991."
It is illustrated.

178.   Suggs, Henry Lewis, ed. *The Black Press in the Middle West, 1865-1985.* Westport,
CT: Greenwood Press, 1996.

Twelve essays by outstanding historians focus on the development of the Black press
in the Middle West. The history and current status of the Black press in the
following states are discussed: Illinois, Indiana, Iowa, Kansas, Michigan, Oklahoma,
South Dakota, and Wisconsin.

179.   Thompson, Julius E. *Black Press in Mississippi, 1865-1985.* Gainesville: University
of Florida Press, 1993.

In this well-documented study, the history and development of the Black press,
including newspapers, magazines, newsletters, radio and television from 1865 to
1985 in Mississippi, is presented. Thompson organizes this study around ten major
areas relative to the Black press: development; content; advertising; economics of
publishing; role of politics, economic affairs, social conditions, radio, and television.

180.   Wilson, Clint C. *Black Journalism in Paradox: Historical and Current Perspectives
and Current Dilemmas.* Westport, CT: Greenwood Press, 1991.

African American journalists of every generation have encountered professional
problems related to race. The study focuses on African American journalists who
have successfully overcome problems related to race in their profession through
strength of character and exceptional job performance.

Television

181.   Cosby, Camille O. *Imageable Influence: The Self-Perception of Young African-
Americans.* Washington, DC: University Press of America, 1994.

Research has shown that the images presented on television affect the self-perception
of children and young adults. This study explores the effect of selected Black
television shows on the self-perception of a selected group of Black young adults.

182.   Gray, Herman. *Watching Race: Television and the Struggle for Blackness.*
Minneapolis: University of Minnesota Press, 1995.

How is Blackness represented on commercial television? How is Black politics
portrayed in commercial culture? This highly theoretical study examines the
relationship of Black expressive culture to Black productions on commercial
television.

183.   Ross, Karen. *Black and White Media: Black Images in Popular Film and Television.*
        Cambridge, MA: Polity Press, 1996.

        Concerned primarily with popular media, this study: (1) traces the history of Black
        images used in television and motion pictures from the earliest years of each media
        to the 1990s; (2) identifies the provenance of particular types of characterizations
        which have been historically allocated to Black actors; and (3) discusses ways in
        which modern Black media practitioners are trying to subvert this racist iconography.

Radio

184.   Cantor, Louis. *Wheelin' on Beale: How WDIA Memphis Became the Nation's First
        All-Black Radio Station and Created the Sound That Changed America.* New York:
        Pharos Books, 1992.

        In 1949 WDIA in Memphis switched from white programming to all-Black
        programming and became the first radio station in the United States with a format
        designed exclusively for Blacks. Cantor, a white announcer at the station, documents
        the story of WDIA, which played a major role in the careers of such Black performers
        as B.B. King, Bobby Blue Bland, Johnny Ace and Roscoe Gordon.

185.   Durham, Richard. *Richard Durham's Destination Freedom: Scripts from Radio's
        Black Legacy, 1948-50.* Edited by J. Fred McDonald. New York: Praeger, 1989.

        From June 27, 1948 through August 1950, "Destination Freedom," a radio series was
        broadcasted over WMAQ, the Chicago-owned-and-operated station of the National
        Broadcasting Company. The Sunday half-hour feature programs, presenting dramatic
        profiles of great African Americans, were written by African American dramatist
        Richard Durham. Over a two-year period, Durham produced ninety-one different
        scripts. Selected scripts from "Destination Freedom" are presented in this work.

186.   Ely, Melvin Patrick. *The Adventures of Amos 'n' Andy: Social History of an
        American Phenomenon.* New York: Free Press, 1992.

        "Amos 'n' Andy" was one of the most popular radio, and later television, shows in
        American entertainment history. White and Black audiences were faithful listeners
        and viewers to the shows. Author Ely presents a well-researched history of this
        radio/ television series.

187.   Newman, Mark. *Entrepreneurs of Profit and Pride: From Black Appeal to Radio
        Soul.* New York: Praeger, 1988.

        Black-appeal radio is defined as programming and advertising designed specifically
        for Black audiences. This study examines, using historical and communications
        methodology of inquiry, the origin and development of Black-appeal radio.

COLLECTIVE AND INDIVIDUAL BIOGRAPHICAL WORKS

188.   Burns, Ben. *Nitty Gritty: A White Editor in Black Journalism.* Jackson: University Press of Mississippi, 1996.

Between 1941 and 1977, white journalist Ben Burns worked on Black publications: *The Chicago Defender, Ebony, Jet, Sepia,* and *The Chicago Daily Defender.* Burns relates his unique experiences as a white minority journalist in Black journalism.

189.   Gilliam, Dorothy Butler. *Interviews with Dorothy Gilliam.* Recorded by Donita Moorhus for The Washington Press Club Foundation as part of its oral history project, "Women in Journalism." Washington, DC: The Washington Press Club Foundation, 1994.

This is a written transcript with newspaper/television reporter Dorothy Butler Gilliam conducted by Donita Moorhus between December 14, 1992 and December 13, 1993. Ms. Gilliam reminisces about her childhood in Memphis in the late 1930s and 1940s; college days at Lincoln (MO) School of Journalism; early work experiences with *The Louisville Defender*, Johnson Publishing Company, Panorama WTTG/TV and later experiences with *The Washington Post*, where she was the first Black reporter.

190.   Hunter-Gault, Charlayne. *In My Place.* New York: Farrar Straus Giroux, 1992.

On January 9, 1961, Charlayne Hunter-Gault and Hamilton Holmes began registering for the Spring semester at the University of Georgia: the first Black students to be admitted to the university in its 176-year history. In this autobiography Hunter-Gault retells significant moments in her life from her childhood years in Due West, South Carolina, in the early 1940s to June 1, 1963, the day she and Hamilton Holmes graduated from the University of Georgia, after two traumatic-filled years of being the first Black students to integrate that university.

191.   Hunter-Gault, Charlayne. *Interviews with Charlayne Hunter-Gault.* Recorded by Mary Marshall Clark for the Washington Press Club Foundation as part of its oral history project, "Women in Journalism." Washington, DC: The Washington Press Club Foundation, 1994.

Five interviews with Charlayne Hunter-Gault, newspaper/television reporter, which were conducted by Mary Marshall Clark between June 15, 1993 and April 6, 1994, are reported on this written transcript. Hunter-Gault talks about her professional life after she graduated from the University of Georgia focusing on her experiences as a reporter for *The New Yorker, The New York Times* and "McNeil-Lehrer News Hour."

192.   Rowan, Carl T. *Breaking the Barriers: A Memoir.* New York: Harper Perennial, 1991.

Seasoned journalist Carl T. Rowan has been Director of the CIA, Ambassador to Finland, and a U.S. Representative to the U.N. Today he is one of the most widely read syndicated columnists in the United States. In this memoir Rowan reminisces and interprets major events in his life from his boyhood in Middle Tennessee as well as the years of his spectacular career in government.

193.   Simpson, Carole. *Interviews with Carole Simpson*. Recorded by Donita Moorhus for The Washington Press Club Foundation as part of its oral history project, "Women in Journalism." Washington, DC: The Washington Press Club Foundation, 1994.

Donita Moorhus conducted nine interviews with radio/television reporter Carole Simpson between October 6, 1992 and June 17, 1994. In this written transcript of those interviews Carole Simpson discusses her childhood in Chicago; life as an undergraduate at the University of Illinois and the University of Michigan; early professional experiences as a radio/television reporter at WBBM-Chicago and WMAQ-TV-Chicago in the 1960s and 1970s; and the professional challenges she faced when she moderated the Presidential Debates in 1992.

194.   Streitmatter, Rodger. *Raising Her Voice: African-American Women Journalists Who Changed History*. Lexington, KY: University of Kentucky Press, 1994.

The lives of eleven outstanding African American women journalists from the nineteenth and twentieth centuries are spotlighted in this collective biography. They are Maria W. Stewart, Mary Ann Shadd Cary, Gertrude Bustill Mossell, Ida B. Wells-Barnett, Josephine St. Pierre Ruffin, Delilah L. Beasley, Marvel Cooke, Charlotta A. Bass, Alice Allison Dunnigan, Ethel L. Payne, and Charlayne Hunter-Gault.

195.   Suggs, Henry Lewis. *P. B. Young, Newspaperman. Race Politics and Journalism in the New South, 1910-1962*. Charlottesville, VA: University of Virginia Press, 1988.

P[lummer] B[ernard] Young was the owner and editor of the Norfolk (VA) *Journal and Guide*, one of the most widely-circulated African American newspapers during the first six decades of the twentieth century, from 1910 until his death in 1962. Against the backdrop of political life in Norfolk and the South, Suggs carefully portrays the life of Young as a conservative Black leader who won the respect of southern whites and Blacks who were sympathetic with his accommodationist views.

196.   Thompson, Julius E. *Percy Greene and The Jackson Advocate: The Life and Times of a Radical Black Newspaperman, 1897-1997*. Jefferson, NC: McFarland, 1994.

Percy Greene, editor of *The Jackson (Mississippi) Advocate* from 1939 to 1997, was, perhaps, the most influential Black journalist in Mississippi of his generation. In this biography, journalism historian Julius Thompson carefully analyzes Greene's life from his youth in the late 1890s to his death in 1997. Greene's intellectual development as a conservative as well as his advocacy of conservative views are scrutinized by Thompson.

197.   Waters, Enoch P. *American Diary: A Personal History of the Black Press.* Chicago: Path Press, 1987.

A leading Black newspaper journalist for more than three decades, Enoch P. Waters, formerly executive editor of *The Chicago Defender*, "tells all" in this revealing biographical narrative. Waters shares his intimate knowledge of many personalities and the events which have influenced Black American life for the last fifty years.

198.   Wolsley, Roland E. *Black Achievers in American Journalism.* Nashville: James C. Winston Pub. Co., 1995.

Since 1827, when *Freedom's Journal* was launched, Black Americans have distinguished themselves as journalists working on Black-owned and white-owned publications. Substantial profiles of twenty outstanding living and deceased Black journalists are presented in this collective biography. Profiles of the following journalists are included: Robert S. Abbott; Samuel Cornish; Martin R. Delany; Frederick Douglass, W. E. B. DuBois; T. Thomas Fortune; Charlayne Hunter-Gault; James Weldon Johnson; John H. Johnson; William H. Lee; Carl Murphy; John H. Murphy, Jr.; Gordon Parks; Ethel Payne; John B. Russwurm; John H. Sengstacke; Chuck Stone; Susan L. Taylor; William Monroe Trotter; Samuel Ringgold Ward; Ida B. Wells-Barnett.

SELECTED PERIODICAL ARTICLES

199.   Bishop, Ed. "Ch. 2's Donn Johnson Talks About TV News, Politics, Management and Racial Bias (Interview)." *St. Louis Journalism Review* 26;1881 6-9.

Articulate and outspoken Donn Johnson, Black anchor on St. Louis' KTVI (Channel 2), candidly discusses Blacks and the television industry in St. Louis in this transcribed interview. Johnson observes that there is no meaningful representation of the Black community in management of newsrooms in St. Louis. He asserts that Blacks, because of their Eurocentric and Afrocentric educational backgrounds, would bring a broader perspective to news management than white managers who have only an Eurocentric educational background.

200.   Brown, Carolyn M. "The Changing Face of the Magazine Industry," *Black Enterprise* 26:1; 78-86, August 1995.

Blacks represent less than 1% of the editorial pool at some 7,000 national magazines published in the United States. Most of these Black editors and reporters are employed by three Black-owned magazines; *Ebony, Black Enterprise*, and *Essence*.

In this article Brown discusses the lack of adequate representation of Blacks and other minorities on the editorial staff of white-owned magazines and the effect on the magazine industry.

201.   Cosby, Bill. "50 Years of Blacks on TV (50th Anniversary Issue)." *Ebony* 51:1; 215-218.

Bill Cosby, an outstanding television producer and actor, discusses the status of Blacks on television. He observes that Blacks are not portrayed realistically on television and wonders why Blacks are not given the opportunity to write and produce television shows.

202.   Delaney, Paul. "The Black Vanguard Integrates Newsrooms," *Media Studies Journal*, 11:2; 16-22, Spring 1997.

With degrees from many of the best schools of journalism in the United States, Black journalists have fought to integrate newsrooms of most of the country's major newspapers.   In this article Delaney documents the activities of many Black journalists working in the newsrooms of large metropolitan dailies.

203.   Edmonds, Alfred, Jr., "25 Years of Blacks in Media," *Black Enterprise* 25:12; 104-107, July 1995.

Since 1970, Black ownership of media has been rapidly expanding. A host of Black-owned national magazines have come into existence: *Black Enterprise* (1970); *Essence* (1970); and *Emerge* (1989), to name a few. Black-owned broadcasting and television stations have sprung up in New York, Detroit, Chicago, and Washington, D.C. Edmonds surveys the growth of Black-owned media between 1970 and 1995, but cautions that in 1995 a conservative Congress eliminated a FCC tax provision which was designed to increase minority ownership of broadcast properties.

204.   Fiske, Fred. "Trailblazers Like Wycliff Make the Journey a Little Easier," *The Masthead* 49:3; 12-15.

In 1991 Don Wycliff became editorial page editor of *The Chicago Tribune*. Wycliff has been awarded a Pulitzer Prize and the American Society of Newspaper Editors Distinguished Writing Award for Editorials. Wycliff's achievements and career as a Black journalist are profiled by Fiske in this article.

205.   Fitzgerald, Mark. "Slaves' to Media Masters: Nation of Islam Leader Rips Black Journalists for Selling Out to 'Controlled Press,'" *Editor and Publisher* 29:35; 10-13, August 31, 1996.

Addressing the 1996 Convention of the National Association of Black Journalists (NABJ), Louis Farrakhan called the group's members "slaves" of the owners of the white press. Using several direct quotes from Farrakhan's address, Fitzgerald reports substantively on the speech and the reactions of members of the N.A.B.J.

SELECTED DISSERTATIONS

206.   Abernathy, Gloria Eugenia. "African Americans Relationship with Daytime Serials." Ph.D. dissertation, University of Wisconsin-Madison, 1993.

The popularity of daytime serials in the African American community is examined in this study using media and critical cultural studies theoretical frameworks. Face-to-face interviews, using an open-ended questionnaire, were conducted of forty-five African Americans who viewed daytime serials. Some of the findings reported on: (1) criticisms by African American viewers of the characters created to portray African Americans; (2) African American images on television; and (3) the viewing practices of African Americans.

207.   Anthony, Jacqueline. "Black Politicians and the Media: A Content Analysis of Newspaper Coverage of Black State Legislators in the Georgia General Assembly 1983 and 1993 Sessions." Ph.D. dissertation, Georgia State University, 1994.

This study focuses on the news coverage of Black state legislators in the Georgia Assembly during the 1983 and 1993 legislative sessions. A content analysis of the *Atlanta Constitution* was conducted to determine whether the coverage of Black legislators was positive, negative or neutral when compared to the news coverage of white legislators during the two legislative sessions.

208.   Barney, Deborah Verdice Smith. "The Gospel Announcer and the Black Gospel Tradition." Ph.D. dissertation, University of Michigan, 1994.

Gospel announcers on radio today are extremely popular in the Black community. These announcers present programs on more than 500 radio stations throughout the United States. In this study a performance analysis of three gospel announcers is conducted by Barney. The gospel announcers are Al "the Bishop" Hobbs, Delores "Sugar" Poindexter, and Edna Tatum.

209.   Crowder, Ralph LeRoy. "John Edward Bruce and the Value of Knowing the Past: Politician, Journalist, and Self-Trained Historian of the African Diaspora, 1856-1954." Ph.D. dissertation, University of Kansas, 1994.

Crowder documents the life and accomplishments of John Earl Bruce, one of the most active African American newspaper correspondents at the turn of the century. In addition to being a journalist, Bruce was an activist in Republican politics, a popularizer of Black history, and an advisor to Marcus Garvey and the UNIA.

210.   DeSantis, Alan Douglas. "Selling the American Dream: The Chicago Defender and the Great Migration of 1915-1919." Ph.D. dissertation, Indiana University, 1993.

Between 1915 and 1919, an estimated one million African Americans migrated from the rural South to the northern cities in what was called "The Great Migration." *The Chicago Defender*, this study argues, was a major force in influencing African Americans to leave the South. *The Chicago Defender*, according to DeSantis, used three motifs in its "migration campaign": (1) southern discontent; (2) land of hope; and (3) call to action.

211.   Ellis, Charlesetta Maria. "Robert S. Abbott's Response to Education for African Americans via The Chicago Defender, 1909-1940." Ph.D. dissertation, Loyola University of Chicago, 1994.

Robert S. Abbott began publishing *The Chicago Defender* on May 5, 1905. Influenced by Plato, Frederick Douglass and Booker T. Washington, Abbott became the "race orator" of Black journalism. Abbott's education philosophy was based on Platonic idealism and the employment of utilitarianism as a component of the learning process.

212.   Jordon, William George. " 'Getting America Told': The Black Press and Its Dialogue with White America, 1914-1919." Ph.D. dissertation, University of New Hampshire, 1996.

Jordan discusses the role African American newspapers played as a forum for white Americans to address African Americans during World War I. This study is based on a close examination of four weekly African American newspapers (the *Baltimore Afro-American, The Chicago Defender, The Cleveland Gazette,* and *The New York Age*), one monthly magazine (*Crisis*), and samplings of ten other African American newspapers.

213.   Kelley, Venita Ann. "Revealing the Universal Through the Specific in 'A Different World': An Interpretative Approach to a Television Depiction of African American Culture and Communication Patterns." Ph.D. dissertation, University of Kansas, 1995.

Rhetorical styles and interpersonal relations in African American life as depicted in the television show "A Different World" are analyzed in this study. The method of analysis employed is interpretative and African-centered.

214.   O'Brien, Patrick Michael. "MOVE: News Coverage of Confrontations, Philadelphia, 1978-1987: A Cultural Studies Approach." Ph.D. dissertation, University of Iowa, 1992.

This is a case study of local print coverage of MOVE, a Black activist organization, and officials and representatives of the city of Philadelphia between 1978 and 1985. The methodology used in this study was: (1) in-depth interviews; (2) qualitative analysis of news coverage; and (3) a Q methodological multivariate factor analysis of readers' interpretations of the news coverage.

215.   Owens, Reginald Lee. "The African American Press As Response to Oppression: Trends in Formation and Circulation." Ph.D. dissertation, The University of Texas at Austin, 1993.

Owens analyzes the social conditions of African Americans and the resulting relations between various indicators of oppression and formation/circulation figures of African American newspapers between 1900 and 1990. The indicators of oppression used in this study are: Lynchings (1900-1990); Executions (1930-1968); Murder Executions (1930-1968); Rape Executions (1930-1970); Infant Mortality (1915-1968); Maternal Mortality (1915-1968); and Male Deaths (1900-1968).

216.   Stafford, Camilla Vedette. "African American Newscast Presentations and Decision-Making Research: Toward An Integrated Framework." Ph.D. dissertation, The Ohio State University, 1994.

Content analyses, Stafford observes, have shown that presentations of African American newsmakers on newscasts are inadequate when compared to white newsmakers. Stafford seeks to examine the decision-making process which has resulted in poor presentations of African Americans on newscasts. A field study was conducted to ascertain the decision-making process which had been used relative to the presentations of African Americans on newscasts and suggests areas of change.

Black Souls Expressed: Blacks in Folklore

SELECTED REFERENCE SOURCES

217. *Arts of Black Folk Conference for Community Organizations: Presenting African American Folk Arts.* New York: Schomburg Center for Research in Black Culture, New York Public Library, 1988.

This conference, sponsored by New York Public Library's Schomburg Center for Research in Black Culture, was held April 22-23, 1988. This volume includes papers presented on the following topics: "Part I: The Cultural Eye: Documenting and Presenting African American Folk Arts"; "Part II: The Cultural Eye: Reports from the Field"; "Part III: New Horizons"; and "Part IV: Funding African American Folk Arts". Contributors were Robert Baron, Gerold L. Davis, Roland Freeman, Gladys-Marie Fry, Nancy Groce, Bess Lomas Hawes, Sharon V. King, Worth Long, Phyllis M. May-Machunda, Diana Baird N'Diaye, and Beverly Robinson.

218. Boyd, Eddie L., et al. *Home Remedies and the Black Elderly: A Reference Manual for Health Care Providers*, by Eddie L. Boyd, Leslie Ship and Marvie Johnson Hackney. Levittown, PA: Pharmaceutical Information Associates, Ltd.; Ann Arbor, MI: Institute of Gerontology and College of Pharmacy, University of Michigan, 1991.

Aimed at physicians, nurses, and social workers who provide health care for the Black elderly, this manual, based on a study of 50 Black elderly residents of southeastern Michigan who use home remedies, is compendium of Black folk medicine. Included in this work are sections on the use of home remedies and detrimental, as well as therapeutic, effects of many home remedies.

219. Cole, Harriette. *Jumping the Broom: The African American Wedding Planner.* New York: Henry Holt and Company, 1993.

"Jumping the Broom" was a marriage custom practiced by African American slaves. This marriage manual, based on the revered custom, offers practical advice for planning an African American style marriage.

220.   Coleman, Chrisena. *Mama Knows Best: African-American Wives' Tales, Myths and Remedies for Mothers and Mothers-to-Be.* New York: Simon & Schuster, 1997.

This delightful manual of African American folk medicine is aimed at preparing women, psychologically and physically, for pregnancy and motherhood. Some of the tips handed down through generations of Black women about pre-natal care and motherhood are cures for backaches, heartburn, and mood swings.

221.   Davis, Rose Parkman. *Zora Neale Hurston: An Annotated Bibliography and Reference Guide.* Westport, CT: Greenwood Press, 1997.

This is a comprehensive annotated bibliography and reference guide to the works by and about Zora Neale Hurston, early Black folklorist, Harlem Renaissance writer and dramatist. It includes citations to books, dissertations, theses, essays, chapters in books, media, and world wide web sites.

SELECTED TREATISES AND COMMENTARIES

222.   Big Mama. *Them Gospel Songs: Lore of the Black Church Experience.* Text and cover illustrations by Daughter Tray Andrea Redic. Aurora, CO: Published for the Cultural Alliance Foundation by National Writers Press, 1990.

This is a collection of texts and commentaries of gospel songs which originated in a Black church in Quincy, Illinois. They are unique, earthy Black folk expressions illustrating the religious devotion practiced by one Black congregation.

223.   Brown, Sterling. *A Son's Return: Selected Essays.* Edited with introduction by Mark Sanders. Boston: Northeastern University Press, 1996.

Written by the former Howard University literature professor and writer, this collection of essays discusses many aspects of Black folk culture and its perception by white writers and scholars. Among some of the topics discussed are folktales, worksongs, spirituals, and jazz.

224.   Fontenot, Wonda L. *Secret Doctors: Ethnomedicine of African Americans.* Westport, CT: Bergin & Garvey, 1994.

The practice of African American folk medicine is explored in this well-documented study. Focusing on the African American folk medicine system which originated in rural Louisiana since the early eighteenth century, Fontenot discusses: (1) the history of African Americans in rural Louisiana; (2) the historical development of the folk medicine tradition among these African Americans; (3) their oral accounts of the practice of folk medicine; (4) the role of prayer and spiritual beliefs in the healing process; and (5) medical ethnobotany traditions used by practicianers of African American folk medicine.

225.   Green, Danita Roundtree. *Broom Jumping: A Celebration of Love.* Richmond, VA: Entertaining Ideas, Ltd., 1992.

This is a history and guide to the African American marriage custom of "Jumping the Broom." Among the aspects of "Jumping the Broom" discussed are: African origins of "Jumping the Broom"; "The Broom"; "Jumping the Broom for Your Anniversary"; "Broom Jumping and Wedding Record"; and "Jumping the Broom for Your Reunion."

226.   Minton, John. *"Big 'Fraid and Little 'Fraid": An Afro-American Folktale.* Helsinki: Academia Scientiarm Fennica, 1993.

In this lecture presented to the Finnish Academic of Science, Minton discusses the African American folktale *"Big 'Fraid and Little 'Fraid."* This analysis focuses on the variants of the folktale, its origins, the character of the monkey, and other features.

227.   Prahlad, Sw. Anand. *African-American Proverbs in Context.* Jackson, MS: University Press of Mississippi, 1996.

Most studies of African American proverbial speech have been text-based and focused on proverbs as a reflection of African American character. In this seminal study Prahlad seeks to interpret the multiple meanings in African American proverbial speech. The methodology employed in this study includes speech act analysis and performance theory.

228.   Roberts, John W. *From Trickster to Badman: The Black Folk Hero in Slavery and Freedom.* Philadelphia: University of Pennsylvania Press, 1989.

Many earlier researchers and writers have evaluated the African American folk tradition from an Eurocentric perspective. In this study Roberts examines the African American folk hero from the Afrocentric perspective arguing that the folk heroes of African Americans have been largely influenced by African expressive forms. Roberts' discussion of the concept of the "Bad Nigger" is highly original.

229.   Snow, Loudell F. *Walkin' Over Medicine: Traditional Health Practices in African American Life.* Boulder, CO: Westview, 1993.

Snow, who is an anthropologist and professor of pediatrics, gathered information on African American folk medicine from clients at two urban pre-natal care clinics. This fascinating study includes transcribed interviews with informants who have used African American folk medicine, African American faith healers and other practitioners. In his analysis of these interviews, Snow uses an array of sources from the exant literature on African American folk medicine.

230.   Sundquist, Eric J. *The Hammers of Creation: Folk Culture in Modern African-American Fiction.* Athens: University of Georgia Press, 1992.

Using the primary texts of Black writers James Weldon Johnson, Zora Neale Hurston and Arna Bontemps, Sundquist discusses the influence of African American folklore on the works of these writers. The novels discussed are *The Autobiography of an Ex-Colored Man,* by James Weldon Johnson; *Jonah's Gourd Vine,* by Zora Neale Hurston; and *Black Thunder,* by Arna Bontemps.

231.   Turner, Patricia A. *I Heard It Through the Grapevine: Rumor in African American Culture.* Berkeley, CA: University of California Press, 1993.

In the African American community rumors about race relations have existed for four hundred years. This study is devoted to analyzing the historical examples of folk rumor discourse in the African American community as well as contemporary examples.

232.   Wright, Lee Alfred. *Identity, Family and Folklore in African American Literature.* New York: Garland, 1995.

Beginning with slave narratives and continuing to works by contemporary writers, Wright discusses how folklore and the blues have been used to signify meaning in African American literature. The works of such nineteenth century writers as William Wells Brown, Charles Chestnutt and Harriet Jacobs, as well as twentieth century writers Toni Morrison, and Alice Walker, are analyzed.

SELECTED COLLECTIONS OF AFRICAN AMERICAN FOLKTALES

233.   Bennett, John. *The Doctor to the Dead: Grotesque Legends and Folktales of Old Charleston.* Columbia: University of South Carolina Press, 1995.

Originally published in 1946, this unusual collection of twenty-four Gullah folktales were told to writer John Bennett by elderly African American skilled and unskilled workers. Three of the folktales are edited by Bennett and written in a "modified Gullah dialect." Twenty-one of the folktales are rendered by Bennett in "academic English." Bennett's avowed purpose in producing the collection was "to identify and preserve the heart and soul of South Carolina Lowcountry literary tradition."

234.   Hamilton, Virginia. *Her Stories: African American Folktales, Fairy Tales, and True Tales.* New York: Blue Sky Press, 1995.

This award-winning collection of folk narratives spotlights the heroic exploits of African American women. These folktales, fairy tales and true tales were told originally by African American slaves in Louisiana, the Carolinas and the Sea Islands of Georgia.

235.   Lester, Julius. *The Tales of Uncle Remus: The Adventure of Brer' Rabbit.* As told by Julius Lester. Illustrated by Jerry Pinkney. New York: Dial Books, 1987.

Prize-winning author Julius Lester retells forty-eight Uncle Remus tales. Lester relates these tales in "modern contemporary Southern Black English."

236.   Sanfield, Steve. *The Adventures of High John the Conqueror.* New York: Dell, 1992.

High John the Conqueror was the folk hero of African American slaves who embodied their spirit of freedom in the face of adversity. This folk hero is the central character of the sixteen folktales included in this collection.

237.   Satino, Jack. *Miles of Smiles, Years of Struggle: Stories of Black Pullman Porters.* Urbana: University of Illinois Press, 1991.

Black Pullman porters worked on America's trains in the years following the Civil War to the late 1970's. In this Black folk history Black Pullman Porters relate their shared occupational experiences through stories told in interviews conducted by Santino. Through these stories they described their reactions to racism encountered on the job, unionizing, A. Philip Randolph, and their role as porters.

238.   Torrence, Jackie. *The Importance of Pot Liquor.* New York: St. Martin's Press, 1995.

"Pot liquor" was the seasoned liquid which was left over when slaves cooked turnip, mustard, or collard greens, for their masters' family. Slaves added corn meal or flour to "pot liquor" and served it to field slaves and yard slaves. It was very nutritious and strengthened the bodies of slaves. After slavery, African Americans continued to use "pot liquor" as a source of strength and as a cure for some illnesses. Jackie Torrence retells twelve "family" folktales centered around the use of "pot liquor."

SELECTED PERIODICAL ARTICLES

239.   Clark, Eric. "Folklorist Virginia Hamilton Tells the Tale," (Interview), *The Crisis* 103:1; 28-32, January 1996.

Virginia Hamilton, award-winning children's and young adult author, discusses African American folklore which she has used as the basis for several of her stories and novels. In African American folklore, Hamilton observes, there are more folktales about men than women.

240.   Domina, Lynn. "Protection in My Mouf: Self, Voice and Community in Zora Neale Hurston's *Dust Tracks on a Road* and *Mules and Men.*" *African American Review* 31:2;197-209, summer 1997.

Mules and Men, published in 1935, was the result of Hurston's expedition into her native South as an observer and to collect African American folklore. *Dust Tracks on a Road*, released in 1942, was Hurston's autobiography. In this article Domina compares the two works from the perspective of Hurston as an observer and the observed.

241.   Dundes, Alan. "'Jumping the Broom': On the Origin and Meaning of an African American Wedding Custom," *Journal of American Folklore*, 109: 433; 324-329, Summer 1996.

This well-researched article asserts that the wedding custom "Jumping the Broom" did not originate with African American slaves. Dundes presents evidence showing that the wedding custom was practiced by Gypsies in England and Scotland.

242.   Gunn, Giles. "Neglected Resource of Scholarship," *Religion and Culture*, 7; 8-14, Winter 1997.

Using concepts gleaned from Lawrence W. Levine's *Black Culture and Black Consciousness: Afro-American Folk Thought from Slavery to Freedom* (1977), Gunn discusses the importance of the study of African American folk culture as a key to gaining insights into African American history. Because many history scholars have neglected the study of African American folk culture, Gunn contends that many flawed interpretations of African American history have prevailed.

243.   Harris, Trudier. "'The Yellow Rose of Texas': A Different Cultural View (Historical Interpretation of the Folk Song About an Afro-American Woman)," *Callaloo* 20:1; 8-20, Winter 1997.

Was Emily D. West, the heroine of the Texas-Mexican War who inspired the song "Yellow Rose of Texas," white or Black? Using Anita R. Bunkley's novel *Emily, The Yellow Rose* (1989) which portrays Emily as a Black woman, Harris explores the possibility that the folk heroine was a Black woman whose Black husband wrote "The Yellow Rose of Texas."

244.   Jordan, R. A. And DeCaro, F. "'In this Folklore Land': Racy, Class Identity, and Folklore Studies in Louisiana," *Journal of American Folklore* 109:435; 31-59, Winter 1996.

Much of Louisiana folklore has African American roots. However, through the years, since 1892 when the Louisiana Folklore Society was founded, white folklorists have had an identity problem relative to exploring African American folklore in the state. In this article, Jordan and DeCaro traces the history of this problem citing folklorists and issues involved.

245.   Meisenhelder, Susan. "Conflict and Resistance in Zora Neale Hurston's *Mules and Men*," *Journal of American Folklore* 109:433; 267-299, Summer 1996.

Meisenhelder critically examines Hurston's use of folklore in *Mules and Men* (1935). Hurston, Meisenhelder observes, "carefully arranged folktales (in the book) ...to reveal complex relationships between race and gender in Black life."

246.   Ogunleye, Tolagbe. "African American Folklore: Its Role in Reconstructing African American History," *Journal of Black Studies* 27:4; 435-456, March 1997.

African American folklore, consisting of myths, storytelling, recollections, ballads, songs, and rap, provide rare insights into the history of Black Americans. Ogunleye asserts, however, that many of America's folklorists have presented a racist view of African American folklore by collecting and publishing folktales and songs which reinforce negative stereotypes of African Americans.

247.   Patton, Phil. "Mammy: Her Life and Times," *American Heritage* 44:5; 78-86, September 1993.

The history of the legendary "Mammy" is traced in this illustrated article. Patton discusses the origin of the legend in the antebellum South, the changes that have occurred in the legend with each generation, and its contemporary critics.

248.   Sullivan, C. W. "'Jumping the Broom': A Further Consideration of the Origins of an African American Wedding Custom," *Journal of American Folklore* 110:436; 203-4, Spring 1997.

In response to Alan Dundes' article on "Jumping the Broom" (see citation 241), more evidence is presented to prove that this wedding custom did not originate with African Americans. Sullivan cites and discussed documented occasions when this custom was practiced in Wales.

SELECTED DISSERTATIONS

249.   Boynton, Maria. "Springtown, New Jersey: Exploration in the History and Culture of a Black Rural Community." Ph.D. dissertation, University of Pennsylvania, 1986.

This study examines the use of tradition in a rural Black community. Over a five-year period, Boynton's methodology conducted oral historical, folkloristic and archival fieldwork. She concluded that Blacks in Springtown did use their African legacy in their activities, but also incorporated other elements from diverse sources in their ongoing folklife.

250.   Brown, Cecil Morris. "Stagolee: From Black Bully to Culture Hero." Ph.D. dissertation, University of California, Berkeley, 1993.

Brown traces the career of African American folk hero Stagolee from the Mississippi levee in the last decades of the nineteenth century to the popular culture of today. During his research Brown unearthed a murder report dated December 25, 1895, which proved that there is historical fact for the folklore surrounding Stagolee's death. The study concludes with a comparison of folk hero Stagolee to Bobby Seale, Malcolm X and Adam Clayton Powell.

251.   Gray, Pearl Spears. "African American Folkloric Form and Function in Segregated One-Room Schools." Ph.D. dissertation, Oregon State University, 1985.

To what extent was the West African Folkloric oral tradition used by African American women teachers who taught in one-room schools in the South in the early 1900s? This study seeks to explore this question by (1) conducting personal interviews with informants; (2) examining archival materials, newspapers, books and records; and (3) making telephone contacts.

252.   Jackson, Joyce Marie. "The Performing Black Sacred Quartet: An Expression of Cultural Values and Aesthetics." Ph.D. dissertation, Indiana University, 1988.

Black sacred quartets have been a tradition in the Black community since the 1880s. These quartets have significantly influenced Black minstrels and early rhythm and blues. This study analyzes the traditional Black sacred quartet and attempts to define its role in Black folklife.

253.   McGregory, Jerrilyn M. "'There Are Other Ways to Get Happy': African American Urban Folklore." Ph.D. dissertation, University of Pennsylvania, 1992.

McGregory presents an ethnographic analysis of African American urban folk culture as a communal experience. Focusing on the cultural parameters which shape African American folklife in Philadelphia, this study examines African American folklife in stylized sports, recreation and carnival plays.

254.   Peterson, Elizabeth Eleanor. "Trickster and Trader: Portrait of an Entrepreneur." Ph.D. dissertation, Indiana University, 1990.

Robert "Bud" Garrett is an African American junkyard owner, musician, and craftsman in Free Kill, Tennessee, a rural Black community. This study focuses on specific folk traditions of the Trickster practiced by Garrett in his entrepreneurial activities.

255.   Seward, Adrienne Lanier. "Early Black Film and the Folk Tradition: An Interpretive Analysis of the Use of Folklore in Selected All-Black Cast Feature Films." Ph.D. dissertation, Indiana University, 1985.

The use of African American folklore in *Hallelujah* (1929), *The Green Pastures* (1936), and *The Blood of Jesus* (1941) is analyzed in this study. Seward demonstrates that stereotypes of Blacks in these films are exoteric manifestations of white folklore about Blacks. A comparison is made between the use of Black folk tradition in the films with its actual occurrence in the cultural context.

256.   Tetzlaff, Monica Maria. "Cultivating A New South: Abbie Holmes Christensen and the Reconstruction of Race and Gender in a Southern Region, 1852-1938." Ph.D. dissertation, University of Pennsylvania, 1995.

Abbie Holmes Christensen was an early folklorist who authored one of the first books on African American folklore, *Afro-American Folklore: Told 'Round Cabin Fires on the Sea Island of North Carolina* (1892). This study examines Christensen's life and career as a folklorist, activist and educator.

Signifying and Rapping: Blacks in Linguistics

SELECTED REFERENCE WORKS

257.   Anderson, Monica. *Black English Vernacular: From "Ain't" to "Yo' Mama" - The Words Politically Correct Americans Should Know*. Highland City, FL: Rainbow Books, 1994.

This is a dictionary of commonly used words and phrases by African Americans for generations. Arranged alphabetically by word or phrase, each entry includes: (1) the word or phrase; (2) phonetic spelling; (3) the Standard English synonym; and (4) an example illustrating its use.

258.   Major, Clarence, ed. *Jubal to Jive: A Dictionary of African American Slang*. Revised ed. New York: Viking Penguin, 1994.

Writer Clarence Major has produced a revised edition of his *Dictionary of African American Slang (1970)* under a new title. This revised edition, Major states, "has at least three times the number of entries than were in the original edition." Entries are arranged alphabetically by word or phrase. Each entry contains the following items; (1) the word or phrase; (2) abbreviation for the part of speech; (3) decade or decades when the word or phrase was used; (4) definition; (5) abbreviations of cited sources in the "Explanatory Notes" where the word or phrase can be found.

259.   Smitherman, Geneva. *Black Talk: Words and Phrases from the Hood to the Amen Corner*. Boston: Houghton Mifflin, 1994.

Smitherman, an outstanding Black linguist, presents the lexical core of words and phrases in African American English in this dictionary. Arranged alphabetically by word or phrase, each entry includes: (1) the word or phrase; (2) definition; and (3) cross references to other entries, when appropriate.

260.   Young, Savannah M. *English: An African American Handbook: The Guide to the Mastery of Speaking More and Better English*. St. Louis: Miller-Young, 1996.

Written for African Americans whose first language is Black English dialect, this guide is designed to assist them in mastering standard American English. Sections of this self-help textbook are devoted to: (1) the history of Black English dialect; (2) a comparison of words and sounds in Black English dialect and standard American English; (3) an explanation of the parts of speech in standard American English; and (4) exercises in speaking standard American English.

SELECTED TREATISES, STUDIES AND COMMENTARIES

261.   Bailey, Guy, et al., eds. *The Emergence of Black English: Text and Commentary.* Amsterdam; Philadelphia: Benjamin Publishing Co., 1991.

The recorded texts of interviews of twelve former slaves, which are presented in this work, who were born between 1844 and 1861 are the basis for these commentaries by nine linguists on the emergence of Black English. The nine commentaries are: "Speaking of Slavery: the Historical Value of the Recordings with Slaves," by Paul D. Escott; "Slave Narratives, Slave Culture, and the Slave Experience," by Joe Graham; "Song, Sermons, and Life Stories: the Legacy of the Ex-Slave Narrative," by Jeutonne P. Brewer; "The Linguist Value of the Ex-Slave Recordings," by Michael Montgomery; "Representativeness and Reliability of the Ex-Slave Materials, with Special Reference to Wallace Quarterman's Recording and Transcript," by John R. Rickford; "Is Gullah Decreolizing? Comparison of a Speech Sample of the 1930s with a Sample of the 1980s," by Salikoko S. Mufwene; "The Atlantic Creoles and the Language of the Ex-Slave Recordings," by John Holm; "Liberian Settler English and the Ex-Slave Recordings: A Comparative Study," by John Victor Singler; "There's No Tense Like the Present: Verbal -S Inflection in Early Black English," by Shana Poplack, Sali Tagliamonte.

262.   Butters, Ronald R. *The Death of Black English: Divergence and Convergence in Black and White Vernaculars.* New York: Lang, 1989.

In this study Butters challenges the thesis that contemporary Vernacular Black English is divergent from other vernacular varieties of English. This work is a critique of the "divergent hypothesis."

263.   Ewers, Traute. *The Origin of Black English: "Be" Forms in HooDoo Texts.* New York: Mouton deGruyter, 1995.

Ewers focuses on the origins of Black English and its subsequent development from the 1930s to 1970. This study is based on selected interviews with Black HooDoo doctors in the North and the South which were conducted by a white priest named Hyatt between the 1930s and 1970. Using data gleaned from these interviews, Ewers investigates the use of the verb "to be" by Black HooDoo doctors.

264.   Holloway, Joseph and Vass, Winifred. *The African Heritage of American English.* Bloomington: Indiana University Press, 1993.

In this study Holloway and Vass set out to show how American English has been enriched by African languages. Using extant scholarship and conducting primary research, the authors identify the Bantu vocabulary content of Gullah; Africanisms of Bantu origin in Black English; Bantu place names in nine Southern states; and Africanisms in contemporary American English.

265. Lee, Carol. *Signifying As a Scaffold for Literary Interpretation: The Pedagogical Implications of an African American Discourse Genre.* Urbana, IL: National Council of Teachers of English, 1993.

In the Black community "signifying" is a traditional form of expression between Black people. "Signifying" can be "loud talking," "rapping," or "testifying." Lee asserts in this highly creative study, which is based on her doctoral dissertation at the University of Chicago, that the skills of expression learned by Black youth in "signifying" can be used as a framework in helping Black adolescents understand literary texts.

266. Lewis, Richard O. *Conventional Functions of Black English in American Literature.* San Francisco: Austin & Winfield, 1997.

In this study Lewis analyzes the components of Black English. He further identifies sixteen conventional functions of Black English and illustrates their use in American literature.

267. Mufwene, Salikoko S., ed. *Africanisms in Afro-American Languages Varieties.* Athens: University of Georgia, 1993.

This volume includes papers presented at the International Round Table on Africanisms in Afro-American Varieties, which was held at the University of Georgia, February 25-27, 1988. The papers focused on Creoles and semi-Creoles which have developed since the seventeenth century as a result of contact of Africans with speakers of European languages. American Black English Vernacular and Gullah are addressed in papers as well as varieties spoken in the Bahamas, the Caribbean and Central and South America.

268. Schneider, Edgar. *American Earlier Black English: Morphological and Syntactic Variables.* Tuscaloosa, AL: University of Alabama Press, 1989.

Schneider's original work on earlier American Black English was published in 1981 in German and was entitled *Morphilogische und Syntaktische Variablem im Amerikanischen Early Black English.* In this work he challenged the Creole hypothesis relative to the origin of American Black English. The present work is a revised and updated translation of the original work and includes developments which have taken place in the study of American Black English since 1980.

269. Sutcliffe, David and Figueroa, John. *System in Black Language.* Philadelphia: Multilingual Matters, 1992.

Sutcliffe and Figueroa examine the development and structure of British Jamaican Creole, the language spoken by persons of Caribbean descent living in England.

British Jamaican Creole, when spoken by the young persons of Caribbean descent, is generally used bilingually with standard or regional English such as London English or Black Country English.

270.   *Verb Phrase Patterns in Black English and Creole,* edited by Walter F. Edwards and Donald Winford. Detroit: Wayne State University Press, 1991.

The thirteen essays in this collection discuss various aspects of grammatical patterns in verb phase constituents of Caribbean Creoles and American Black English. The essays included in this collection are: "General Introduction: Linguistic Relations Between Black English and Caribbean Creoles," by Walter F. Edwards; "Black English: Introduction," by Walter F. Edwards; "A Reexamination of the Black English Copula," by John Baugh; "The Relationship of White Southern Speech to Vernacular Black English," by Walt Wolfram; "The Use of Invariant 'be' with Verbal Predicates in BEV," by John Myhill; "Verb Patterns of Black and White Speakers of Coastal South Carolina," by Patricia C. Nichols; "Copula Variation in Liberian Settler English and American Black English," by John Victor Singler; "Multiple Modals 12 [2] 505 0 in United States Black English: Synchronic and Diachronic Aspects," by Ronald R. Butters; "Creole: Introduction," by Donald Winford; "13 505 0 The Concept "Do" in English and English-Lexicon Creole," by Dennis R. Craig; "On the Infinitive in Gullah," by Salikoko S. Mufwene; "Modality in Jamaican Creole," by Pauline Christie; "A Comparative Description of Guyanese Creole and Black English Preverbal Aspect Marker 'Don'," by Walter F. Edwards; "The Passive in Caribbean English Creole," by Donald Winford; "Focus and Assertion in Jamaican and Barbadian Speech," by Peter Roberts; "Contemporary Source Comparison as a Critical Window on the Afro-American Linguistic Past," by John R. Rickford.

SELECTED PERIODICAL ARTICLES

271.   Koch, Lisa M. And Gross, Alan. "Children's Perception of Black English As a Variable in Intraracial Perception." *Journal of Black Psychology* 23:3, 215-225, August 1997.

The authors report on findings in a survey conducted on African American junior high students to determine their perceptions of Black English. It was revealed that these students had greater appreciation for adults who used Black English than those adults who use Standard American English. By contrast, the authors observed middle-class African American adults who preferred the use of Standard American English by African American adults because they felt it made them more competitive in the workplace.

272.   Lippo-Green, Rosina. "What We Talk About When We Talk About Ebonics: Why Definitions Matter." *The Black Scholar* 27:2, 7-12, Summer 1997.

Lippi-Green discusses the problems involved in giving the variety of English spoken by almost 80% of African Americans a standard definition. Is Ebonics, Black English, Black English Vernacular, or African American Vernacular English?

273. McMillen, Liz. "Linguists Find the Debate Over 'Ebonics' Uninformed: They See
      Black English As a Language Variety and Decry Attacks on Oakland's School
      Board." *The Chronicle of Higher Education* 43:19; A16-A18, January 17, 1995.

      Linguists, McMillen reports, support the Oakland School Board's decision to include
      Black English in the curriculum. Black English, the linguists point out, is not a
      separate language from Standard English, but a separate dialect. It functions with the
      rules of language and could be used to enhance the teaching of Standard American
      English to Black students.

274. Mufwene, Salikoko S. "The Ecology of Gullah's Survival." *American Speech* 72:1;
      69-84.

      Gullah is a Creole dialect which has been spoken by African Americans living on the
      coastal islands off the coasts of northern Georgia and South Carolina for over 400
      years. In this article Linguist Salikoko Mufwene discusses changing economic,
      social, and demographic forces in the region that threaten Gullah's survival as a
      living language.

275. "Oakland Amends Ebonics Resolution." *Black Issues in Higher Education* 13:25;
      29-32, February 6, 1997.

      The Oakland School Board's decision to amend its Ebonics resolution is discussed
      in this article. The reasons for the amended resolution are highlighted as well as
      testimony of Oakland officials before a United Senate subcommittee investigating
      the Ebonics issue.

276. Rickford, John R. "Suite for Ebony and Phonics." *Discover* 18:12; 82-88, December
      1997.

      Focusing on the decision by the Oakland School Board to include Ebonics, linguist
      John R. Rickford describes the negative attitude of the general public. By contrast,
      however, he spotlights quotes from James Baldwin and Toni Morrison praising Black
      English. Finally, Rickford analyzes Black English and finds that it is a highly
      grammatically structured dialect and not a separate language.

277. Smitherman, Geneva. "The Chain Remains the Same: Communicative Practices in
      the Hip-Hop Nation." *Journal of Black Studies* 29:1; 3-26.

      Hip-Hop, according to Smitherman, is a term which symbolizes African American
      communication practices and traditions. In Hip-Hop music, which is rap music,
      African Americans express their struggles and feelings of survival in a predominately
      white society. Rap music becomes a language which reflects the oral tradition of the
      Black cultural evolution.

278. Todd, Leon W. "Ebonics Is Defective Speech and a Handicap for Black Children."
      Education 118:2; 177-181, Winter 1997.

Todd views Ebonics as dysfunctional speech. Putting Ebonics in the curriculum, he believes, just legitimatizes poor language. American society, Todd concludes, is based on Standard English. Placing Ebonics at the center of a child's learning experience will cripple the child in later life.

SELECTED DISSERTATIONS

279.   Boyd, Gwendolyn Aline. "Teacher Attitudes Toward African American Vernacular English: The Relationship to Students' Perceptions of Classroom Climate." Ph.D. dissertation, The University of Memphis, 1996.

The extent of positive and negative attitudes of selected teachers toward African American Vernacular English (AAVE) and their effect on classroom climate were explored in this study. To gather data the following methodology was employed. Seventy-two teachers and five hundred and four students from grades 2 to 6 from seven elementary schools in a large urban city in the South were surveyed. Teachers responded to statements on an attitude survey using the *Language Attitude Scale* in regards to African American Vernacular English (AAVE). Five hundred and four students were asked to complete a short version of *My Class Inventory* to gather information about classroom climate.

280.   Brown, Fahamisha Patricia. "Black Poetry: A Vernacular Art." Ph.D. dissertation. Boston University, 1996.

Brown discusses African American Vernacular speech as a language system available to African American poets. As it is practiced, this language system, Brown observes, provides the African American poet with a base vocabulary, metaphors and style.

281.   Campbell, Kermit Ernest. "The Rhetoric of Black English Vernacular: A Study of Oral and Written Discourse Practices of African American Male College Students." Ph.D. dissertation, The Ohio State University, 1993.

Most research on Black Vernacular English (BVE) has ignored the functions of BVE such as rapping, signifying and mimicry. These functions for BVE speakers are varied and complex. They should be used as an asset, Campbell argues in teaching these speakers academic prose. This study demonstrates that viewing BVE as an asset in the classroom for teaching writing is indispensable for connecting African American students of non-standard dialect backgrounds to the academic community.

282.   Dayton, Elizabeth. "Grammatical Categories of the Verb in African-American Vernacular English." Ph.D. dissertation, University of Pennsylvania, 1996.

Be2, done, bedone, been done, stressed Bin, unstressed Bin and *had* are elements of the African American Vernacular English (AAVE) system of mood modality, tense and aspect. As individual items, the grammatical meaning of these elements has been widely researched. However, ways in which these elements are systematically related are as yet to be determined. This study analyzes 3,610 tokens of these items which were collected in the African American Speech community in Philadelphia.

283.   Green, Lisa J. "Topics in African American English: The Verb System Analysis."
        Ph.D. dissertation, University of Massachusetts, 1993.

This study considers some issues relative to the verb system in African American
English. Among these issues are: (1) the meaning associated with aspectual markers;
(2) the properties of finite and aspectual markers in the context of the principles and
parameters approach of verb raising in Pollock.

284.   Huang, Xiaozhao. "African American English in 'Middletown': A Syntactic and
        Phonological Study with Time-Depth Data to Test the Linguistic Convergence and
        Divergence Hypothesis." Ph.D. dissertation, Ball State University, 1994.

Huang analyzed time-depth data of speech samples for thirty-two African American
subjects, male and female, in Muncie, Indiana, to determine if African American
Vernacular English (AAVE) was converging or diverging with White Vernacular
English (WVE). Sixteen of the samples were taken in 1980 and sixteen were taken
in 1993. The analysis of these samples focused on twenty-three syntactic and five
phonological features. The finding of this study did not support the divergence
hypothesis.

285.   Humber, Toni Cheryl. "A Sociolinguistic Analysis of an Urban Language
        Proficiency Program for African American Students, Grades Kindergarten Through
        Sixth Grade." Ph.D. dissertation, Howard University, 1993.

This study profiles and analyzes the Proficiency in English Program (PEP) used in
the Los Angeles School District for African American children to determine if the
program incorporates sociolinguistic principles into the structure of its program
components. Humber uses two data collection methods: (1) sociolinguistic content
analysis; and (2) a sociolinguistic survey.

286.   Lee, Margaret G. "An Historical, Sematic, and Contextual Analysis of the Lexical
        Borrowing of Black Verbal Expressions in a Mainstream Newspaper." Ph.D.
        dissertation, Indiana University of Pennsylvania, 1997.

The Daily Press is the newspaper of the Virginia Peninsula. This study investigates
57 Black verbal expressions that appeared in 121 articles in *The Daily Press* from
August 17, 1993 to October 14, 1996. The findings revealed that the majority of the
Black expressions originated in the Jazz or Rap eras and were coined words or
multiple-meaning words.

287.   Snyder, Patricia Annedarko Tillman. "Classroom Interactions in Features That
        Contrast African American Language (AAL) and Mainstream American English
        (MAE): A Multilinguistic Perspective of Mediation Strategies." Ph.D. dissertation,
        University of California, Los Angeles, 1995.

Focusing on African American language speakers in elementary school, Snyder administered to the speakers a questionnaire about cognition and language awareness. The speakers were also asked to perform two metalinguistic tasks. The objective of this study was to create a method of data collection which would be useful in assisting African American language speakers in making the transition to Mainstream American English.

Witnessing: Blacks in the Visual Arts

SELECTED REFERENCE WORKS

288. *Gumbo Ya Ya: Anthology of African American Contemporary Artists.* With an introduction by Leslie King-Hammond. New York: Midmarch Arts, 1995.

    Over 162 twentieth-century African American women artists are profiled in this work. Each profile presents the following information about the artist: (1) vital statistics; (2) artist's philosophy as expressed in her work; (3) a commentary on the artist's work and career; (4) illustrations of the artist and a selection of her works; (5) lists of the exhibitions and museums housing her works.

289. Henkes, Robert. *The Art of Black Women: Works of Twenty-Four Artists of the Twentieth Century.* Jefferson, NC: McFarland & Co., 1993.

    A chapter is devoted to each of the twenty-four Black women artists. After presenting a profile of the artist, Henkes critically discussed selected illustrated works. The following facts about the artist are cited in a table at the end of the chapter: (1) career highlights; (2) a list of selected group exhibits; (3) a list of solo exhibits; (4) a bibliography of books, periodicals and catalogues about the artist and her works. The twenty-four artists are: Emma Amos; Camille Billops; Vivian Browne; Nanette Carter; Mary Reid Daniel; Cynthia Hawkins; Clementine Hunter; Lois Mailou Jones; Viola Burley Leak; Norma Morgan; Delilah Pierce; Howardena Pindell; Faith Ringgold; Malkia Roberts; Jewel Simon; Gilda Snowden; Ann Tanksley; Freida High W. Tesfagiorgis; Alma Woodsey Thomas' Adell Westbrook; and Shirley Woodson.

290.   Lewis, Samella. *African American Art and Artists.* (Rev. ed). Berkeley, CA:
       University of California Press, 1994.

       An updated edition of *Art: African American* (1978), this present work presents
       biographies of 176 artists with illustrations of selected works as well as photographs
       of the artists. Artists working between 1865 and 1960 are represented with more
       substantive biographies than artists who were active after 1960.

291.   Perry, Regenia. *Free Within Ourselves: African American Artists in the Collection
       of the National Museum of American Art.* Introduction by Kinshasha Holman
       Cornwell. Washington, DC: National Museum of American Art, Smithsonian
       Institution with Pomegranate Art Books, San Francisco, 1992.

       In 1992 the works of 105 African American artists were represented in the collection
       of the National Museum of American Art (NMAA) in Washington, DC. The works
       of 31 of these artists are included in this volume which was conceived as a
       companion publication to "Free Within Ourselves: African American Artists in the
       Collection of the National Museum of American Art," an exhibition which was on
       display at the NMAA in 1992, and, subsequently, a traveling exhibit to five other
       museums in the United States. A chapter is allocated to each of the 31 artists. Within
       each chapter the life and career of the artist is profiled. Selected works by the artist
       are illustrated and critically discussed. Appended to the main body of the work is
       a relative bibliography, a list of the names of all African American artists who have
       worked in the NMAA, and an index giving name, subject and title access to the
       entire work.

292.   Thomison, Dennis, comp. *The Black Artist in America: An Index to Reproductions.*
       Metuchen, NJ: Scarecrow Press, 1991.

       Reproductions of the works of Black artists in various publications are indexed in this
       unique reference work. Historically, the artists included ranged from Joshua Johnson
       (1790s) to the late 1980s (Richard Hunt). Entries are arranged alphabetically by the
       surname of the artist. The following information is included in each entry: (1) name
       of the artist; (2) year and place of birth; (3) art medium; (4) abbreviation of
       source/sources where biographical information may be found; (5) abbreviation of
       source/sources that have a portrait of the artist; (6) name of the title(s) with the
       abbreviation of source where the reproduction may be found, in some instances the
       shortened name in parenthesis where the work is located; (7) further references.

293.   Willis-Thomas, Deborah. *Black Photographers, 1840-1940: An Illustrated Bio-
       Bibliography.* New York: Garland Publishing Co., 1985.

Sixty-five African American photographers who were active between 1840 and 1940 are included in this bio-bibliography. This work is divided into two sections: "The Photographers" and "The Photography." In "The Photographers" entries are grouped under four historical periods: "I. Daguerreans, 1840-1859," "II. Daguerreans and Photographers, 1860-1899," "III.Photographers, 1900-1919," and "IV. Photographers, 1920-1940." Entries, which are arranged alphabetically by surname within these historical periods, contain the following information: name of photographer; birth and death years; career highlights; principal subjects; photography process; collection(s) housing the photographer's works; selected bibliography. In the section entitled "Photographs" illustrations of photographers' works arranged historically beginning with an illustration of a photograph of J. B. Ball (ca 1880) to an illustration of a photograph taken by Austin Hensen (ca1940).

294.   Willis-Thomas, Deborah. *An Illustrated Bio-Bibliography of Black Photographers, 1940-1988.* New York: Garland Publishing Co., 1989.

A continuation of *Black Photographers, 1840-1940: An Illustrated Bio-Bibliography* (1985), this volume focuses on Black photographers who were active between 1940 and 1988. In part one entitled "The Photographers" entries are arranged alphabetically by the surname of the photographer. Typical entries include the following items: (1) photographer's name; (2) birth years or active years; (3) biographical profiles; (4) listing of public repositories housing the works of the photographer; (5) list of selected exhibits; and (6) a selected bibliography. Part two, "Photographs" are reproductions of the photography of photographers included in the work.

SELECTED TREATISES AND COMMENTARIES

295.   Callahan, Nancy. *The Freedom Quilting Bee.* Tuscaloosa, AL: University of Alabama, 1987.

Quilting has been a folk art practiced among African American women in Alabama's Black Belt since the 1840s, when slave women began creating quilts for themselves and their mistresses and masters. At the height of the Civil Rights Movement in 1965, however, Francis X, a white Episcopal minister deeply involved in the Movement, led several African American women who lived in the Black Belt, in establishing The Freedom Quilting Bee Cooperative, which has become a successful and nationally-known business venture. Nancy Callahan tells the story of The Freedom Quilting Bee and its development as a component of the Civil Rights Movement in Alabama, spotlighting in substantive profiles of many of the women quilters and their work.

296.   Driskell, David, ed. *African American Visual Aesthetics: A Postmodernist View.* Washington, DC: Smithsonian Institution, 1995.

This collection of essays examining postmodernism in African American art were presented as a series of papers at a symposium in the Spring of 1991 at the Hirshorn Museum and Sculpture Garden at the Smithsonian Institution. The five essays are "Introduction: The Progenitors of a Postmodernist Review of American Art," by David Driskell; "The Global Village of African American Art," by Keith Morrison; "Living Fearlessly with and within Difference(s): Emma Amos, Carol Ann Carter, and Martha Jackson-Jarvis," by Sharon Patton; "The African American Aesthetic and Postmodernism," by Ann Gibson; "African American Artists and Postmodernism: Reconsidering the Careers of Wilfredo Lam, Romare Bearden, Norman Lewis, and Robert Coles Colescott," by Lowery Stokes Sims; "African American Postmodernism and David Hammons: Body and Soul," by Richard Powell.

297.   Pindell, Howardina. *The Heart of the Question: The Writings and Paintings of Howardina Pindell.* New York: Midmarch Press, 1997.

Howardina Pindell is an African American painter who has worked in several arts administration positions. Presently, she is Professor of Art at Yale. In this collection of writings, which includes essays and pages from her diaries, Pindell shares her concerns on several aspects of art and the art world. Among some of these concerns are: "racism against Blacks in the art world"; "censorship of art by right-wing groups"; and "restrictions on women in the art world."

298.   Powell, Richard J. *Black Art and Culture in the Twentieth Century.* London: Thames and Hudson, 1997.

Duke University Art Historian Richard Powell discusses brilliantly the social and political contexts in which art in the Black Diaspora have developed in the twentieth century. More than 170 illustrations, 31 in color, and concise biographies of 160 Black artists, mostly African American, are included in this work.

299.   Vlach, John M. *By the Work of Their Own Hands: Studies in Afro-American Folklife.* Charlottesville, VA: University of Virginia Press, 1991.

In this collection of essays John Vlach, a leading folklorist, discusses three aspects of African American folk art: (1) folk art; (2) artisans' lives; and (3) block building. Although the discussion focuses on African American artisans and folk artists in the Antebellum South, Vlach does consider the work of some artists who were productive in the latter nineteenth and early twentieth centuries such as gravestone sculptor William Edmondson and blacksmith Philip Simmons.

SELECTED BIOGRAPHICAL WORKS

300.   Bearden, Romare and Henderson, Harry. *A History of African American Artists: From 1792 to the Present.* New York: Pantheon, 1993.

Substantive biographical and critical commentaries with reproductions on more than thirty African American artists and African Americans who promoted art are presented in this important work. All biographees were born before 1925 and lived between 1792 and 1990. Biographees are grouped under six categories: "The Late Eighteenth and Nineteenth Centuries"; "The Twenties and the Black Renaissance"; "Emergence of African Artists During the Depression"; "The Naive, Self-Taught Artists"; "Art Departments in African-American Colleges and Universities"; and "Post-World War II African-American Artists."

301.   Ketner, Joseph D. *The Emergence of the African American Artist: Robert S. Duncanson, 1821-1872.* Columbia: University of Missouri Press, 1993.

Robert S. Duncanson has recently been heralded as one of the leading American landscape painters of the nineteenth century. Based on new information, this critical biography reconsiders the life and work of this, all but forgotten, pioneer African American artist who won national and international acclaim in the nineteenth century for his landscape paintings.

302.   Kirschke, Amy Helene. *Aaron Douglas: Art, Race and the Harlem Renaissance.* Jackson: University Press of Mississippi, 1995.

Aaron Douglas is frequently referenced as "the Father of African American art." Douglas was one of the first African American artists to incorporate African art into his work. This is the first book-length biography to treat Aaron Douglas's life and work. In the first half of this work Douglas' life is chronicled from his birth in Kansas to his years in Harlem where he became one of the leading artists of the Harlem Renaissance. The second half of this work is devoted to an analysis of Aaron Douglas' work.

303.   Powell, Richard J. *Homecoming: The Art and Life of William H. Johnson.* Washington, DC: National Museum of Art, Smithsonian Institution; New York: Rizzoli, 1991.

For many years William H. Johnson was almost invisible to the mainstream art world. In 1971, one year after his death, however, a retrospective exhibition of William H. Johnson's work at the National Museum of American Art at the Smithsonian Institution gave the artist national exposure. Richard J. Powell's well-researched biography, which was published on the occasion of the exhibition, traces Johnson's life from Florence, South Carolina, where he was born in 1901 to the Harlem years of the 1920 and 1930s to the post-World War II years in Scandinavia from 1940 to the 1960s and to his last years of confinement for mental illnesses. Powell includes in this biography 170 reproductions of Johnson's work, a chronology of selected exhibits, a list of collections housing Johnson's work, and an extensive bibliography of works on Johnson.

304.   Schwartzman, Myron. *Romare Bearden, His Life & Art.* Foreword by August
        Wilson. New York: Abrams, 1990.

In his foreword, playwright August Wilson credits the art of Romare Bearden with
causing him to perceive " black life on its own terms, on a grand and epic scale, with
all its richness and fullness." As this magnificent biography unfolds one wonders
how many other Black people have, like Wilson, been so profoundly influenced by
Bearden's art. In six chapters of this work, Schwartzman, who interviewed Bearden
every Tuesday morning for six years, perceptively discusses stages in Bearden's life
from his childhood in Charlotte, North Carolina, where he was born in 1911, through
his years in Pittsburgh in the 1920s , Harlem of the 1940s and his subsequent years
of development as an artist. 150 color reproductions as well as 100 black and white
reproductions, which graphically document Bearden's artistic development, are
critically discussed by Schwartzman.

305.   Smith, Glen R. and Kenner, Robert. *Discovering Ellis Ruley.* Preface by Barbara A.
        Hudson. Foreword by Robert Farris Thompson. Introduction by Gerald C. Wertkin.
        Art Study Essay by Stacy Hollander and Lee Kogan of the Museum of American Folk
        Art. New York: Crown Publishers, 1993.

Ellis Ruley was an African American folk artist who died at the age of 77 in Norwich,
Connecticut, where he had lived his entire life. Although he began painting late in
life, few people, outside of his immediate family, were aware of his artistic pursuit.
In 1950 Ruley began to exhibit his work. His paintings were well received. In this
work the authors relate the facts about Ruley's life that they were able to research in
a brief biographical profile. However, authorities on folk art and art history discuss
in three essays the significance of Ruley's art.

306.   Willis, Deborah, Ed., *J. P. Ball, Daguerrean and Studio Photographer.* New York:
        Garland Publishers, 1993.

James P. Ball was one of the pioneering photographers in antebellum America.
Between 1845, when he opened his first daguerreotype studio in Cincinnati, until
1904, when he died in Seattle, Ball made magnificent strides in developing the art of
photography. This first book published on James P. Ball includes: (1) a biography
of Ball's life; (2) a catalogue of reproductions of Ball's daguerreotypes and
photographs which are housed in public and private collections; and (3) a
reproduction of Ball's anti-slavery pamphlet which was published in 1855 and
entitled *Ball's Splendid Mammoth Pictorial Tour of the United States Comprising
Views of the African Slave Trade.*

CATALOGUES OF SELECTED EXHIBITIONS

307.   Benberry, Cuesta. *Always There: The African American Presence in Quilting.* Louisville: Kentucky Quilt Project, 1992.

Published in conjunction with the installation of "Always There: The African Presence in Quilting," an exhibition which was on view at The Museum of History and Science, Louisville, Kentucky, February 7 through March 31, 1992, this catalogue was authored by the exhibition curator, Cuesta Benberry. It contains a history of African American quiltmaking from the late eighteenth century to the 1990s focusing on major African American quiltmakers and many unique quilting techniques. There are color reproductions of 35 outstanding quilts and an extensive bibliography.

308.   *Black Photographers Bear Witness: 100 Years of Social Protest.* (Essays by) Deborah Willis, Howard Dodson, III. Williamstown, MA: William College Museum of Art, 1989.

"Black Photographers Bear Witness: 100 Years of Social Protest" was one of three exhibitions organized by the Williams College Art Museum to celebrate the centennial of the graduation in 1889 of the college's first Black graduate, Gaius Charles Bolin. Deborah Willis' essay is a brief, but informative, history of African American photographers from 1840 to the late 1980s. Howard Dodson, III, surveys in a brief essay the history of Black protest in the United States between 1883 and the late 1980s. Twelve Black photographers, who were active between 1840 and the 1980s, are profiled with reproductions of their photographs or photographic reconstructions. A checklist of the works by the twelve photographers in the exhibition is included.

309.   *Harlem Renaissance: Art of Black America.* Introduction by Mary Schmidt Campbell. Essays by David Driskell, David Levering Lewis, and Deborah Willis Ryan. New York: Studio Museum of Harlem/Harry Abrams, 1987.

This catalogue of "Harlem Renaissance: Art of Black America," a massive exhibition organized and presented at the Studio Museum of Harlem in 1987, presents a panoramic view of the flurry of artistic activity which flourished in Harlem during the 1920s. Mary Schmidt Campbell's introduction is an enlightening survey of the Harlem Renaissance years spotlighting major artists and events. "Harlem My Home," which is an excerpt from David Levering Lewis' *When Harlem Was in Vogue* (1981) is a running commentary on the period by a knowledgeable observer illustrated by reproductions of James Van Der Zee photographs. David Driskell's essay "The Flowering of the Harlem Renaissance: the art of Aaron Douglas, Meta Warrick Fuller, Palmer Hayden and William H. Johnson" is a critical assessment with color reproductions of the works of these artists and Deborah Willis Ryan's essay "James Van Der Zee" is an authoritative assessment of the great Harlem photographer. A chronology of the Harlem Renaissance and an extensive related bibliography are also included.

310.   Kelley, Harmon. *The Harmon and Harriet Kelley Collection of African American Art Exhibit.* Organized by Douglas K. W. Hyland; Essays by Gylbert Coker and Corrine Jennings. San Antonio: San Antonio Museum of Art, 1994.

Harmon and Harriet Kelley were inspired to begin collecting African American art in 1987 after viewing "Hidden Heritage: African American Art, 1800-1950," an exhibition at the San Antonio Art Museum. This is the catalogue of the exhibition, which represents the fruits of the collecting efforts of Harmon and Harriet Kelley, since 1987 which was installed at the San Antonio Art Museum of Art and on display from February through April 1994. Three informative essays on African art are presented in this catalogue. Gylbert Coker's "Nineteenth-Century African American Art" is a historical survey of African American art and artists which considers the works of such artists in the exhibition as Joshua Johnson (? - 1830?); Robert S. Duncanson (1821-1872); Grafton Brown (1841-1918); Edward Bannister (1828-1901); Henry Ossawa Tanner (1859-1937); Charles E. Porter (1847-1943); and Laura Wheeling Waring (1887-1948). "Twentieth Century Artists," by Corinne Jennings, critically discusses the works of such artists in the exhibition as Hale Woodruff, Elizabeth Catlett, Charles Alston, Palmer Hayden, Archibald Motley, Jr., Irene Cook, Eldzier Cortor, Jacob Lawrence, William H. Johnson, and Romare Bearden. In "American Art and the Black Folk Artist" Gylbert Coker focuses on the following artists who had works in the exhibition: Frank Jones, Thornton Deal, William Traylor, Clementine Hunter, John Coleman, Joseph E. Yokum, Sister Gertrude Morgan, and Minnie Evans.

311.   Reynolds, Gary A. and Wright, Beryl J. *Against the Odds: African American Artist and the Harmon Foundation.* With Essays by David Driskell, et al. Newark, NJ: Newark Museum, 1987.

From 1922 to 1967, when the Harmon Foundation closed, it had been the leading supporter of African American art in the United States. "Against the Odds: African American Artists and the Harmon Foundation" is the exhibition which was organized by the Newark Museum where it was on display January 15 to April 15, 1990. As a traveling exhibition it was displayed at the Gibbs Museum of Art in Charleston, South Carolina, May 7 to July 9; 1990; and The Chicago Cultural Center, July 28 to September 29, 1990. In this catalogue of the exhibition seven illuminating essays are presented discussing various aspects of the Harmon Foundation involvement in the support of African American art. These essays are "The Harmon Foundation in Context," by Beryl J. Wright; "An Experiment in Inductive Service," by Gary A. Reynolds; "The Mental Property of the Nation," by Beryl J. Wright; "Mary Beattie Brody and the Administration of the Harmon Foundation," by David Driskell; "In Search of a People's Spirit," by Clement Alexander Price; "William H. Johnson and the Harmon Foundation," by Richard J. Powell; "Photography and the Harmon Foundation," by Deborah Willis; and "American Critics and the Harmon Foundation Exhibitions," by Gary A. Reynolds. Over 101 illustrations of the art work in the exhibition are included as well as photographs of the participating artists.

312. *Rhapsodies in Black: Art of the Harlem Renaissance.* [Exhibition devised and selected by Richard J. Powell and David A. Bailey.] London: Hayward Gallery: Institute of International Visual Arts; Berkeley: University of California Press, 1997.

This exhibition, which opened at London's Hayward Gallery, was on display from June 16 through August 17, 1997. The works of such Harlem Renaissance artists as Richmond Barthe', Aaron Douglas, Meta Warrick Fuller, Sargent Johnson, William H. Johnson, and Augusta Savage are included. This catalogue of the exhibition featured the following essays: "Re-birth of a Nation," by Richard J. Powell; "Voodoo MacBeth," by Simon Callow; "Like a Gypsy's Daughter: or Beyond the Potency of Josephine Baker Eroticism," by Andrea D. Barnell; "Paul Robeson and the Problem of Modernism," by Jeffrey C. Stewart; "Modern Tones," by Paul Gilroy; "Still," by Martina Attille; and "Harlem on Our Minds," by Henry Louis Gates, Jr.

313. Robinson, Jontyle Theresa and Greenhouse, Wendy. *The Art of Archibald Motley, Jr.* With an introduction by Floyd Coleman. Chicago: Chicago Historical Society, 1991.

The Art of Archibald Motley, Jr. was the catalogue for the exhibition of this great artists' works. Organized by the staff of the Chicago Historical Society, the exhibition was on display at the Chicago Historical Society from October 23, 1991 through March 17, 1992. Thereafter the exhibition went on tour to The Studio Museum of Harlem, New York City, April 5 - June 10, 1992; High Museum\Georgia Pacific Gallery, Atlanta, Georgia, June 29 - September 25, 1992; and the Corcoran Gallery of Art, Washington, DC, October 10, 1992 - January 3, 1993. Two informative commentaries on Motley's life and work are included in this catalogue: Jontyle Theresa Robinson's "The Life of Archibald Motley, Jr."; and Wendy Greenhouse's "Motley's Chicago Context: 1890-1940." In the catalogue of the exhibition color reproductions of sixty-nine works are presented with critical commentaries. Other items included in the catalogue are: (1) a checklist of other known works; (2) chronology of the artist's life; (3) selected list of exhibitions; and (4) bibliography of works cited.

314. Robinson, Jontyle T., et al. *Bearing Witness: Contemporary Works by African American Women Artists.* With contributions by Maya Angelou, Thetoba Hayes Benjamin, Pearl Cleage, Johnetta Betsch Cole, M. Akura McDaniel, Beverly Guy-Sheftall, Lowery Stokes Sims and Judith Wilson. New York: Spelman College, Rizzoli Publications, 1996.

Showcasing the works of twenty-five African American Women artists, this is the catalogue of the first major exhibition installed at Spelman College's Museum of fine Arts. Brief biographies of the artists are included. Among the notable essays in this catalogue are "Warrior Women," by Beverly Guy-Sheftall; "Triumphant Determination: The Legacy of African American Women Artists," by Tritoba Hayes Benjamin; "African American Women Artists: Into the Twenty-First Century," by Lowery Stokes Sims, and "Hagar's Daughters: Social History, Cultural Heritage, and Afro-U.S. Women's Art," by Judith Wilson.

315.   Wardlaw, Alvia J. *The Art of John Biggers: View from the Upper Room.* With essays by Edmund Barry Gaither, Alison de Lima Greene and Robert Farris Thompson. Houston: Museum of Fine Arts, in association with Harry N. Abrams, 1995.

The Art of John Biggers: View from the Upper Room is the catalogue for the exhibition of the same name which was organized by the staff of the Museum of Fine Arts, Houston, and The Hampton University Museum. The exhibition was on display at the Museum of Fine Arts, Houston, April 2 - April 28, 1995 and thereafter, as a traveling exhibition was on tour to: North Carolina Museum of Art, Raleigh, North Carolina, October 15, 1995 - January 14, 1996; Wadsworth Athenaeum, Hartford, Connecticut, May 19 - August 25, 1996; Hampton University Museum, October 6 - December 20, 1996; Museum of Fine Arts, Boston, Massachusetts, January 24 - April 20, 1997. John Biggers' life and work are discussed in essays by four authorities on African American art. The essays are "Metamorphosis: The Life and Art of John Biggers," by Alvia J. Wardlaw; "John Biggers: A Perspective," by Edmund Barry Gaither; "John Biggers: American Muralist," by Alison de Lima Greene; "John Biggers 'Shotguns' of 1987: An American Classic," by Robert Farris Thompson. The catalogue for the exhibition describes 127 works. Most works are illustrated in color and black and white reproductions. Included in the catalogue is a chronology of John Bigger's life, a selected exhibition history and a selected bibliography.

316.   Wheat, Ellen Harkins. *Jacob Lawrence: American Painter.* With a contribution by Patricia Hills. Seattle: University of Washington in association with the Seattle Art Museum, 1986.

Published on the occasion of the Jacob Lawrence Exhibition at the Seattle Art Museum, July 10 through September 7, 1986, this work provides a comprehensive overview of Lawrence's life and career. Patricia Hill's "Jacob Lawrence's Expressive Cubism" is a critique on one aspect of the artist's work since the mid-1930s. Seasoned art historian Ellen Harkins Wheat discusses Lawrence's life and works.

SELECTED PERIODICAL ARTICLES

317.   Coleman, Floyd. "Down Home and Uptown: Archibald Motley, Jr and the Evolution of African American Art." *American Heritage* 46:1; 18-25, March 1995.

The paintings of Archibald Motley, Jr., Coleman observes, are realistic and capture the essence of African American urban life. Motley's place in the evolution of African American art is discussed by Coleman in this substantive assessment of Motley's work and career.

318.   Coleman, Floyd and Bruce, Jeffrey. "Two Decades of Momentous Change: 1976-1996." *The International Review of African American Art* 13:2; 29-65, Spring 1996.

The years between 1976 and 1996 marked, according to the authors, "an unparalleled period of development in African American visual arts." A chronology of events which occurred during these years that illustrate dynamic changes in the growth of visual arts among African Americans is presented.

319.   Dalton, Karen C.C. "The Past Is Prologue But Is Pastiche Progress? A Conversation." *The International Review of African American Art* 14:3; 17-30, Summer 1997.

Art historian Michael Harris and art curator Lowery Sims discuss "black collectibles" or "black memorabilia" and the psychological effects that these stereotypical and derogatory depictions have on African Americans today. Much of the "black memorabilia" in existence today was produced during the last decades of the 19th century and the early decades of the 20th century: a period when American politicians and intellectuals were using social Darwinism to prove that African Americans were mentally and morally inferior.

320.   Hewitt, M. J. "Vital Resources." *The International Review of African American Art* 14:2; 19-46, Spring 1997.

It is estimated that there were approximately 800 African American art galleries in the United States in 1995. In this article, Hewitt discusses: (1) early efforts to create exhibit space for African American artists; (2) philanthropic support; (3) attempts by African Americans to organize their own galleries; and (4) the contemporary scene by surveying the activities of several African American-owned galleries.

321.   Kirschke, Amy Helene. "The Depressed Murals of Aaron Douglas: Radical Politics and African American Art." *The International Review of African American Art* 12:4; 18-29, Fall 1995.

The murals painted by Aaron Douglas during the Harlem Renaissance are critiqued by Kirschke. Douglas, Kirschke observes, experimented with color, Cubism, and African art in creating highly innovative works. These murals express Douglas' vision of African American history.

322.   McEvilley, Thomas. "The Missing Tradition." *Art in America* 85:5; 78-87, May 1997.

The city of Atlanta sponsored two African American art exhibitions during the summer of 1996 as components of the Cultural Olympiad. One exhibition, which was entitled "Souls Grown Deep: African American Vernacular Art," included 300 works of art from over 40 contemporary African American artists in the Southeast and was on display at the Atlanta City Hall. Simultaneously, a second exhibition entitled Thornton Dial: Remembering the Road," which included 75 relief paintings by Thornton Dial, a self-taught African American artist, was on display at the Michael C. Carlos Museum at Emory University. McEvilley critiques on both exhibitions in this illustrated article and concludes that the works contained in them represent a force that has been overlooked in American art.

323.   Mercer, Valerie J. "Chiaroscuro: Black Artists in the City of Light, 1945-1965." *American Art* 14:2; 3-8, Spring 1997.

Opened in April 1997, the Hampton University Museum has been heralded by art historian David Driskell as a world class facility. Richelle Payne describes the physical layout of the building; discusses the construction costs; cites some of the outstanding works of art it houses; and interviews Jeanne Zeidler, the Museum's Director.

324.   Weathers, Diane. "Images of An Era, 1976-1996." *The International Review of African American Art* 13:2; 13-28, Spring 1996.

Through interviews with several artists, art historians, art collectors, and arts administrators, Weathers assesses the evolution of the African American art scene from 1976 to 1996. Among the art personalities interviewed were June Kelly, Benny Andrews, Edmund Barry Gaither, Faith Ringgold, Thelma Golden, and Raymond Saunders.

325.   Ziedler, Jeanne. "Reflections on 20 years of *IRAAA*: A Conversation with Samella Lewis." *The International Review of African American Art* 13:2; 4-12, Spring 1996.

Samella Lewis was the founder of *The International Review of African American Art (IRAAA)*. In this article Jeanne Ziedler, Director of Hampton University Museum and publisher of *IRAAA*, interviews Samella Lewis about the early years of the *IRAAA*.

SELECTED DISSERTATIONS

326.   Chappell, Brenda Joyce. "The Consciousness of African American Women Artists: Rage, Activism and Spiritualism (1860-1930). Interdisciplinary Implications for Art Education." Ph.D. dissertation, The Ohio State University, 1993.

African American women artists, Chappell asserts , are, for the most part, excluded from art curricula/textbooks, because most contemporary theories in art education explain the content of African American women's art. This study examines the potential for including African women artists in art textbooks and art curricula.

327.   Drake, Lois Margaret. "Black and White Children's Art: A Cultural Comparison."
        Ph.D. dissertation, University of California-Irvine, 1985.

        In this study Drake tests the historical assertions which claim that differences exist
        between African American art and Euro-American art.   These differences,
        presumedly, are in expression of emotion, self-concept, human involvement, and
        color use. Drake conducted a comparative study of 80 Black children and 71 white
        children in kindergarten classes by asking each class to do the same drawing task.
        The drawings were then labeled and analyzed by Drake.   Each teacher was
        interviewed by Drake about each child's family's history.

328.   Gedeon, Lucinda Heyel. "A Study in Patronage of African American Art, 1776-
        1976." Ph.D. dissertation, University of California, Los Angeles, 1989.

        Gedeon observes that African American artists and artisans have been producing
        artistic works since the United States came into existence. In this study Gedeon
        examines the political and social forces which have influenced the patronage of
        African American artists and artisans from 1776 to 1976.

329.   Hollingsworth, Charles Henry, Jr. "Victor Lowenfeld and the Radical Landscape of
        Hampton Institute [University] During His Tenure (1939-1946)." Ph.D. dissertation,
        The Pennsylvania State University, 1990.

        Victor Lowenfeld, an Austrian Jew who fled Hitler's wrath, taught in the Art
        Department at Hampton Institute [University] from 1939 to 1946. Lowenfeld, while
        at Hampton, influenced a generation of African American art students which included
        such outstanding artists as John Biggers and Samella Lewis. This study, which is
        written in the format of a play, dramatically documents Lowenfeld's contributions
        to art education at Hampton and the development of African American art.

330.   Thomas, Floyd Robert, Jr. "Cultural Conservation Through the Preservation of
        Material Culture--The Representation of Black Artists in Mainstream Museum."
        Ph.D. dissertation, University of Kansas, 1989.

        Thomas examines a variety of factors which have affected the low representation of
        African American artists in the nation's mainstream art museums. He concludes by
        suggesting remedial action that can be taken to insure that these museums will reflect
        more accurately the cultural diversity of the American art experience.

331.   Powell, Richard J. "William H. Johnson: Expressionist and Artist of the Blues
        Aesthetic." Ph.D. dissertation, Yale University, 1988.

        In this study Powell examines Johnson's life and career in an attempt to articulate his
        artistic motives and mechanisms. Johnson's art is analyzed in the context of his life
        focusing on how such factors as environment, artistic milieu and his state of mind
        influenced his creative acts.

332. Rogers, Paul A. "Race and the Discourse of Nature in the Art of the Americas, 1850-1965." Ph.D. dissertation, Yale University, 1993.

Visual objects, Rogers argues, have played a key role in the historical formation of African American subjectivity. By closely examining nineteenth and twentieth century images, Roger attempts to demonstrate how race implicated itself in visual modernism.

Greasepaint and Other Things: Blacks in the Performing Arts

SELECTED REFERENCE WORKS

333.   Bogle, Donald. *Blacks in American Film and Television: An Encyclopedia*. Fireside edition. New York: Simon and Schuster, 1989.

This comprehensive reference source on Black Americans in motion pictures and television is arranged in three major sections: "Movies," "Television," and "Profiles." The sections "Movies" and "Television" are prefaced with historical essays and followed by sub-sections of title entries, arranged alphabetically, to movies or television shows. In each entry are the following items: (1) title; (2) years of production/release; (3) credits; and (4) synopsis of the movie or television show with illustrations. In the "Profiles" entries are arranged alphabetically by surname and contain the following information: (1) name; (2) birth and, if applicable, death dates; (3) photograph of performer; (4) overview of television/or film career; and (5) television/or movie credits. There is a title/performer index to the entire work.

334.   Gray, John, comp. *Blacks in Film & Television: A Pan African Bibliography of Films, Filmmakers & Performers*. Westport, CT: Greenwood Press, 1990.

Containing 5789 citations, this is an extensive bibliography on Blacks in film and television in the Black Diaspora. Unannotated entries are arranged in numerical sequence under the following six broad headings: "I. Cultural History and Arts"; II. African Film"; III. Black Film in the Diaspora: Europe, The Caribbean and Latin America"; IV. Black Film in the Diaspora: United States"; "V. Blacks in American Television and Video"; and "VI. The Black Performer." Citations are to books, periodical articles, newspaper articles, media materials, and clipping files in special collections. The two appendixes are devoted to reference works and film resources respectively. Four separate indexes provide access to the entire work by artist, title, subject, and author.

335.   Mapp, Edward. *Directory of Blacks in the Performing Arts*. 2nd. ed. Metuchen, NJ: Scarecrow Press, 1990.

This second edition of this reference source includes approximately 300 new entries on Black performing artists and updated entries on the 850 artists who were in the first edition (1978). Arranged alphabetically by surname each entry contains the following information: (1) name of performer; (2) area of performing speciality; (3) date and place of birth and death, if appropriate; (4) education; (5) honors; and (6) professional credits.

336.   Peterson, Bernard L. *A Century of Musicals in Black and White: An Encyclopedia of Musical and Stage Works By, About and Involving Blacks.* Westport, CT: Greenwood Press, 1993.

Providing information on more than 1200 musicals by, about and involving Blacks, this comprehensive reference work covers the years from 1873 to 1992. Included in this work are musicals or musical shows: (1) about Blacks; (2) with at least one Black performer; and (3) Black songwriters or librettists. The types of musical shows represented are tent and outdoor shows; vaudeville shows; operettas; musical comedies and farces; musical plays; musical spectacles; reviews; cabaret and night club shows; children's musicals; musical skits; one-act musicals; one-man shows; one-woman shows; and dance reviews. Arranged alphabetically by title of the musical, each entry contains fourteen items of information. These items are: (1) title of musical; (2)other titles, if applicable; (3) inclusive dates of musical's performance history; (4) genre of the musical; (5) length of musical; (6) author(s) of books(s) scripts, lyrics; and composer of music; (7) title and author of original work; (8) circumstances which led to the writing of the musical, (9)significance of the musical; (10) synopses of the plot; (11) production history; (12) title of songs; (13) location of published and unpublished librettos, scores, and recordings; and (14) sources of important commentary or criticism about the show or musical. The work has three indexes: "Name Index"; "Song Index"; and "General Index."

337.   Peterson, Bernard L. *Contemporary Black Playwrights and Their Plays: A Biographical Directory and Dramatic Index.* Foreword by James V. Hatch. Westport, CT: Greenwood Press, 1988.

This reference source provides information on more than 700 contemporary African American resident dramatists, screenwriters, radio and television scriptwriters, musical theater collaborators, and other originators of theatrical or dramatic works which were produced between 1950 and 1988. All playwrights or originators of dramatic works must have; (1) had works published since 1950; (2) been living in 1950; or (3) been born after 1950. Arranged alphabetically by surname, each entry contains: (1) name of the playwright; (2) biographical sketch; (3) an annotated list of representative plays. A title index provides access to all works cited in the main body of the work.

338.   Peterson, Bernard L. *Early Black American Playwrights and Dramatic Writers: A Biographical Directory and Catalog of Plays, Films and Broadcast Scripts.* New York: Greenwood Press, 1990.

Information on 218 pioneering Black American playwrights, screenwriters, and other originators of dramatic works which were written or produced in the United States or Europe prior to 1950 is presented in this work. In the main section of this work, which includes information on 136 authors, entries are arranged alphabetically by surname and include the following items: (1) name; (2) a biographical sketch; (3) a list of published works by the author; and (4) an annotated list of theatrical productions of the authors works. Information on the remaining 82 writers is found in Appendix A: "Other Early Black American Playwrights and Their Plays"; and Appendix B: "Additional Musical Librettists and Brief Descriptions of Their Shows." Appendix D is titled "A Chronology of Plays and Dramatic Works Classified by Genre." A separate title index as well as a general index provide excellent access to the entire work.

339.   Sampson, Henry T. *Blacks in Black and White: A Source Book of Black Films.* 2nd edition. Metuchen, NJ: Scarecrow Press, 1995.

This is the most comprehensive reference source on all-Black films and the Black independent film industry which flourished between 1910 and 1950. Chapters 1 through 6 are devoted to essays and commentaries on the independent Black film industry and individual independent Black filmmakers. Chapter 7 presents synopses of films produced by independent Black filmmakers and all-Black films produced by white filmmakers between 1910 and 1950. Biographical sketches of all independent Black filmmakers are presented in Chapter 8. The appendixes list: (1) all-black films produced in the United States before 1960; (2) a partial list of individuals and organizations which produced all-Black films between 1910 and 1950; and (3) motion picture theaters catering to Black patrons between 1910 and 1950.

MOTION PICTURES

Selected Treatises and Commentaries

340.   Cripps, Thomas. *Making Movies Black: The Hollywood Movie Message from World War II to the Civil Rights Era.* New York: Oxford University Press, 1993.

The United States reacted to nazism in Germany during World War II with a new liberal attitude toward its race problem. Hollywood executives, like most decision-makers, adopted more liberal racial policies, especially towards Black Americans. In this study, Thomas Cripps, Black film historian and critic, discusses the growing status of Blacks in the motion picture industry from World War II to the Civil Rights Era of the 1950s highlighting such landmark motion pictures featuring Black Americans as "The Negro Soldier," "Pinky," "Home of the Brave," and "No Way Out."

341.   Dash, Julie, et al. *Daughters of the Dust: The Making of an African American Woman's Film.* New York: New Press, 1992.

When "Daughters of the Dust," a motion picture written and directed by African American woman filmmaker Julie Dash, was released in 1992, it received rave reviews from film critics. It is the heart-warming story of an African American Gullah family living on a sea-island off the coast of Georgia at the turn of the century preparing to move to the mainland. This volume, which includes a script of the motion picture, presents the commentaries on the film by Dash, Toni Cade Bambara, Greg Tate, and Bell Hooks. A list of awards which the motion picture has received and a filmography of Julie Dash are in the appendixes.

342.   Diawara, Manthia, ed. *Black American Cinema.* New York: Routledge, 1993.

The nineteen essays in this collection discuss Black film from two perspectives. Twelve essayists attempt to develop a Black film aesthetic. Six essayists explore issues related to Black spectatorship.

343.   George, Nelson. *Blackface: Reflections on African Americans and Movies.* New York: HarperCollins, 1994.

Focusing on Black Americans in the motion picture industry from 1963 to 1994, this is a personal memoir by a perceptive, experienced commentator on Black Americans in the industry during the thirty-one year period.

344.   Guerrero, Ed. *Framing Blackness: The African American Image in Film.* Philadelphia: Temple University, 1993.

In this important study Guerrero critically discusses the history of the changing images of Blacks in films from the dehumanizing, racist stereotypes which appeared in "Birth of a Nation" (1915) to the realistic portrayal of Blacks as evidenced in such films as "Malcolm X" (1992). Guerrero cites cultural, racial, political, fiscal and artistic forces which have influenced the changing image of Blacks in motion pictures over the seventy-seven-year period.

345.   Harris, Erich L. *African-American Screenwriters Now: Conversations with Hollywood's Black Pack.* Los Angeles: Silman-James Press, 1996.

Harris, a very productive African American screenwriter, interviews 13 successful African American screen and television writers about the art, craft, and commerce of writing for television and motion pictures as well as being an African American in these areas of the performing arts. The writers are Dwayne Johnson-Cochran, Charles Burnett, Rusty Cundieff, Carol Munday Lawrence, Eric Daniel, Julie Dash, Robert Townsend, Michael Dinwiddie, Lawrence Andries, Tim Reid, Yvette Lee-Bowser, Carl Franklin and Jeanne Williams.

346.   Jones, G. William. *Black Cinema Treasures: Lost and Found.* Foreword by Ossie Davis. Denton, TX: University of North Texas Press, 1991.

From 1910 to the early 1950s, a host of Black-audience motion pictures were produced by an all-Black segment of the motion picture industry. This segment included Black writers, actors, and distributors. In 1983 copies of many of these all-Black films were discovered among other highly-flammable nitrate-stock films in a Tyler, Texas warehouse. These Black films became known as "The Tyler, Texas Black Film Collection." In this fascinating work G. William Jones relates the story of the restoration of these motion pictures and presents biographical sketches of Black filmmakers. Each of the twenty-five motion pictures in the Collection is described with a synopsis, photographs and listings of credits and costs.

347. Lee, Spike. *By Any Means Necessary: The Making of "Malcolm X."* With Ralph Wiley. New York: Hyperion, 1992.

The many problems which filmmaker Spike Lee endured in producing and directing the film entitled "Malcolm X" are discussed by Lee in this autobiographical account. The script of the film, an introduction by novelist Terry McMillan, and Ossie Davis' Eulogy of Malcolm X are included.

348. Lee, Spike. *The Films of Spike Lee: Five for Five.* [essays by Terry McMillan, et al.] Photographs by David Lee. Foreword by Melvin Van Peebles. New York: Stewart, Tabori, 1991.

Published in 1991 after he had directed and produced his first five films, this book, Spike Lee states in his introduction, was a "good idea to take a quick pause for the cause and look back as we move ahead to the next five." The five films are discussed in essays by outstanding writers/critics, with photographs by brother David Lee. The essays are "Thoughts on 'She's Got To Have It," by Terry McMillan; "Programming with 'School Daze,'" by Toni Cade Bambara; "'Do the Right Thing': Film and Fury," by Nelson George; "One Meaning of 'Mo' Better Blues," by Charles Johnson; and "'Jungle Fever': or Guess Who's Not Coming to Dinner," by Henry Louis Gates, Jr.

349. Null, Gary. *Black Hollywood from Nineteen-Seventy to Today.* Secaucus, NJ: Carol Publishing Group, 1993.

Null has produced a pictorial history of Black Americans in the motion picture industry covering the years from 1970 to the early 1990s. The reference value of this volume, which has not been indexed, is the large number of photographs of scenes from motion pictures casting Black Americans.

350. Reid, Mark. *Redefining Black Film.* Berkeley: University of California Press, 1993.

This study discusses films produced by Blacks from 1900 to 1990. Reid defines two types of Black films: Black commercial films and Black independent films. Black commercial films, Reid asserts, are directed, written and produced by Blacks, but distributed by whites. Black independent films are written, produced, directed, and distributed by Blacks.

351.   Rhines, Jesse A. *Black Film, White Money.* New Brunswick, NJ: Rutgers University Press, 1996.

Rhines critically discusses Black involvement in the motion picture industry from 1915 to the mid 1990s. Blacks, according to Rhines, have taken advantage of internal forces within the industry as well as outside forces to advance. In spite of progress made by Blacks in the industry over the last eighty years, Rhines observes that Blacks still face problems related to: (1) Black filmmakers obtaining funding for their film projects; (2) Black women in the industry; and (3) employment discrimination.

352.   Walker, Alice. *The Same River Twice: Honoring the Difficult; A Meditation on Life, Spirit, Art, and the Making of the Film, "The Color Purple," Ten Years Later.* New York: Scribner, 1996.

The motion picture "The Color Purple," based on Alice Walker's novel of the same name, received eleven Academy Award nominations. Despite this acclaim, Walker and the film were attacked bitterly. This memoir, which includes entries from Walker's personal journals, correspondence, published essays and articles, spans the years from 1984 to 1995 and relates facts about the controversy surrounding the film. The original screenplay which Walker wrote for the film, but was not used by Director Steven Spielberg, is published here for the first time.

Selected Biographical Works

353.   Bergman, Carol. *Sidney Poitier.* New York: Chelsea House Publishers, 1988.

Sidney Poitier's acting career in motion pictures began in the 1950s when Hollywood began giving Blacks serious roles. He starred in such motion pictures as "The Defiant Ones," "Blackboard Jungle," and "In the Heat of the Night." In 1964 Sidney Poitier won an Oscar as Best Actor for his role in "Lillies of the Field." In this biography author Bergman traces Poitier's life from his youth in the Bahamas, where he was born in 1927, through his years as one of the foremost film actors of our time.

354.   Bogle, Donald. *Dorothy Dandridge: A Biography.* New York: Boulevard Books, 1997.

In 1965 Dorothy Dandridge became the first Black woman nominated for an Academy Award as the Best Leading Actress. To many Black Americans Dorothy Dandridge was the first authentic movie goddess of color. Prize-winning film historian Donald Bogle has gone beneath the surface to produce this perceptive new biography of the magnificent Black actress.

355.   Jackson, Carlton. *Hattie: The Life of Hattie McDaniel.* Lanham, MD: Madison Books, 1996.

Hattie McDaniel, who won an Oscar for Best Supporting Actress for her role in "Gone With the Wind," was the first Black American to win an Academy Award. In this well-researched biography Jackson recreates the life of this outstanding Black actress who paved the way for other Black actors/actresses.

356.   Parish, James. *Today's Black Hollywood.* New York: Pinnacle Books, 1995.

Parish has written substantive biographical sketches of sixteen contemporary, successful Black Americans in motion pictures and television. The subjects of these biographical sketches are Halle Berry, Bill Cosby, Lawrence Fishburne, Whoopi Goldberg, Whitney Houston, Janet Jackson, Spike Lee, Eddie Murphy, John Singleton, Will Smith, Wesley Snipes, Tina Turner, Denzel Washington, Damon Wayans, and Oprah Winfrey. Also included in this work is "Today's Black Hollywood Filmography."

357.   Parish, James. *Whoopi Goldberg: Her Journal from Poverty to Megastardom.* Secaucus, NJ: Carol Publishing Co., 1997.

Whoopi Goldberg was born in 1955 in New York City with the name of Caryn Johnson. In ninth grade she quit school and began taking drugs. Sometime later she moved to San Diego, with her daughter from her marriage to a drug counselor, and began honing her comedic talents. Under the guidance of Mike Nichols she appeared on Broadway in a successful one-woman show. Although Whoopi won a nomination for an Academy Award in the role of Celie in the film version of Alice Walker's novel "The Color Purple," she did not receive the Oscar. However, she did receive the Oscar for her role in "Ghost." Parish has written a well-researched behind-the-scenes biography of this dynamic Black megastar.

358.   Strode, Woody and Young, Sam. *Coal Dust: An Autobiography.* Lanham, MD: Madison Books, 1990.

Woody Strode, a former football teammate of Jackie Robinson at UCLA in the late 1930s, played professional football in Canada and was a professional wrestler before he became a character actor in motion pictures in 1941. In this candid autobiography, Strode relates his life story focusing on his days as a professional athlete and a motion picture actor who appeared in 57 movies, three television movies and thirteen television series between 1941 and 1985.

TELEVISION

Selected Treatises and Commentaries

359.   Gray, Herman. *Watching Race: Television and the Struggle for Blackness.* Minneapolis: University of Minnesota Press, 1995.

Gray analyzes such Black-centered television shows as "The Cosby Show," "Frank's Place," "In Living Color," and "Saturday Night Live" as examples of television's attempts to represent Blackness in popular culture. Although the Black characters in these shows are considered "safe" for white audiences, Gray contends that they are stereotypical for Black audiences. Gray suggests that such Black characters might be catalysts for producing more authentic Black characters in future television productions.

360.   Hill, George and Moon, Spencer. *Blacks in Hollywood: Five Favorable Years in Film and Television, 1987-1991.* Los Angeles: Daystar Publishing Company, 1992.

The years between 1987 and 1992 marked a period of progress for Blacks in television and motion pictures. In this period history, Hill and Moon chronicle the advances made by Blacks in television and motion pictures during these years by presenting: (1) reviews of television shows and television series with Blacks as major performers; (2) reviews of significant motion pictures with Blacks playing major roles; and (3) listings of Blacks as nominees and winners of Academy Awards, Emmy Awards, and NAACP Image Awards.

361.   Jhally, Sut and Lewis, Justin. *Enlighten Racism: The Cosby Show: Audiences and Myth of the American Dream.* Boulder, CO: Westview, 1992.

The Cosby Show has become one of the most widely viewed shows in recent television history. Unlike Black TV sitcoms of the 1970s, The Cosby Show presents Black comedic characters with dignity and humanity. Some viewers of The Cosby Show argue that it does not present a realistic portrayal of the lives of Blacks in America. Other viewers maintain that The Cosby Show offers an abundance of Black culture. In this study Jhally and Lewis surveyed viewer reaction to The Cosby Show by conducting in-depth discussions with 52 small focus groups in Springfield, Massachusetts.

Selected Biographical Works

362.   Bly, Nellie. *Oprah! Up Close and Down Home.* New York: Kensington Publishing Corp., 1993.

In 1976 Oprah Winfrey was a cub newscaster while attending Tennessee State University, on a local Nashville television station. Today Oprah is hailed as "The Queen of Talk-Shows." In this candid autobiography Oprah recalls the significant events of her childhood, her early years in television, and her experience as a talk-show host.

363.   Nichols, Nichelle. *Beyond Uhra: "Star Trek" and Other Memories.* New York: Putnam, 1994.

For thirty years Nichelle Nichols has been Lieutenant Uhra, a commanding officer on "Star Trek." Nichols was the first Black American woman to have a continuing major role on television. In this autobiographical narrative Nichols describes her childhood in Chicago, young adult years as a dancer, and years as a motion picture and television actress focusing on her tenure on "Star Trek."

THE THEATER

Selected Treatises and Commentaries

364.   Flowers, H. D., II. *Blacks in American Theater History: Images, Realities, Potential.* Edina, MN: Burgess International Group, 1992.

This highly original study traces the involvement of Blacks in American theater history from 1700 to 1991. Dr. Flowers focuses on legitimate drama, minstrel and musical shows, and the professional, community, children's and university theaters among Black people. The study embraces the following subjects: (1) white playwrights and their plays involving Blacks, 1700-1910; (2) white playwrights and Negro characters; (3) Black playwrights and Black theater; (4) minstrels and musical shows; (5) the Black actor; (6) the Little Theater Movement; and (7) the educational theater movement. A chronology of Blacks in the American Theater covering the years 1767 to 1991 is included.

365.   Fraden, Rena. *Blueprints for a Black Federal Theater, 1935-1939.* New York: Cambridge University Press, 1994.

There were seventeen Black units established in the Federal Theater Project (FTP) between 1935 and 1939. These units and the plays they produced were influenced by: (1) the administrators of The Project; (2) the input of Black Intellectuals; (3) Black actors who worked on The Project; and (4) the preferences of Black audiences. In this study Fraden discusses the cultural politics which shaped the activities of these units of the FTP during its four years of existence.

366.   Gill, Glenda E. *White Grease Paint on Black Performers: A Study of the Federal Theater, 1935-1939.* New York: P. Lang, 1988.

At the suggestion of the esteemed Black actress Rose McClendon, seventeen Black units of the Federal Theater Project (FTP) were established which gave employment to 851 Blacks out of a total of 12,000 employees of the FTP. This study documents Black involvement in the FTP by focusing on six Black actors and theatrical personnel whose careers illustrate the impact which the FTP had on the development of the Black theater.

367.   Riis, Thomas Laurence. *Just Before Jazz: Black Musical Theater in New York, 1890-1915.* Washington, D.C.: Smithsonian Institution Press, 1989.

Between 1890 and 1915, Black performers presented more than 30 musical shows in Black New York neighborhoods and on Broadway. Among these productions were "The Policy Players" (1899); "The Sons of Ham" (1900); "In Dahomey" (1903); and "The Southerners" (1904). Riis discusses in this study this exciting period of Black musical shows. He describes Black musicals produced on and off-Broadway.

368.   Sanders, Leslie C. *The Development of Black Theater in America: From Sundown to Selves.* Baton Rouge: Louisiana State University Press, 1989.

What is a "Black stage reality?" How has it been developed? Through an analysis of the plays of Black playwrights, Willis Richardson, Randolph Edmonds, and Ed Bullins, Leslie Sanders attempts to define "Black stage reality?" and discusses how it has been created by these playwrights and other Black playwrights in their plays.

369.   Tanner, Jo A. *Dusky Maidens: The Odyssey of the Early Black Dramatic Actresses.* Westport, CT: Greenwood Press, 1992.

Black actresses in America began performing with The African Company in New York City in 1823. J. O. Tanner documents in this study the evolution of the Black actress on the American stage from the small roles played by Black actresses in antebellum America, to her successes in Black musicals from 1890 to 1915, to her prominence on stage beginning in 1917 with the famed Rose McClendon to the present day.

Selected Biographical Works

370.   Heath, Gordon. *Deep Are the Roots: Memoirs of a Black Expatriate.* Amherst, MA: University of Massachusetts Press, 1992.

In 1945 an immensely talented young Black actor named Gordon Heath played the role of Brett Charles in the award-winning Broadway production of "Deep Are the Roots." Unfortunately, prospects for this exceptional young Black actor, because of racism, looked gloomy. Consequently, Gordon Heath expatriated to Paris in 1948. In spite of his expatriate status, Gordon Heath continued to appear in theatrical productions in the United States and Europe until his death in 1991. In this work, published posthumously. Heath describes his childhood in Manhattan's West Side and experiences in the theater in New York, London, and Paris and his life-long friendships with such theatrical personalities as Owen Dodson, Elia Kazan and Pearl Bailey.

371.   Mortimer, Owen. *Speak of Me As I Am: The Story of Ira Aldridge.* Wangaratta, Victoria, Australia: Published by the author, 1995.

African American Ira Aldridge was one of the most respected Shakespearean actors of the nineteenth century. Using new documents, Mortimer traces Aldridge's life from his birth in New York City in 1807 to his death in 1867, focusing on his years as an actor on the stages of Europe's principal cities.

372.   Simmons, Renee Antoinette. *Frederick Douglass O'Neal: Pioneer of the Actors Equity Association.* New York: Garland, 1996.

In 1964 Frederick Douglass O'Neal was elected President of Actors Equity Association: the first Black American elected to the Association's 11,000 members. This biography examines O'Neal's sixty-year career as an actor, theater organizer, activist and organizational leader.

SELECTED PERIODICAL ARTICLES

373.   Ambush, Benny Sato. "Culture Wars," *African American Review* 31:4; 579-587, Winter 1997.

Ambush reports on Black playwright August Wilson's keynote address delivered at the 11th biennial National Theater Conference on June 26, 1996. The Pulitzer prize-winning playwright asserted that Blacks were different from whites. Black's live in a culture which should not be judged by Eurocentric standards. Wilson advocated federal funding for Blacks to develop a Black theater.

374.   Green, J. Ronald. "Oscar Micheaux's Interrogation of Caricature as Entertainment," *Film Quarterly* 51:3; 16-33, Spring 1989.

For years Hollywood-made motion pictures casting Blacks in stereotypical roles. Through the N.A.A.C.P. and other civil rights organizations, Blacks protested against this practice. Black filmmaker Oscar Micheaux, according to Green, used caricatures of Black stereotypes in his films as a form of protest. Green identifies and discusses caricatures of Black stereotypes in several motion pictures made by Oscar Micheaux.

375.   Harrison, Paul Carter. "The Crisis of Black Theater Identity," *African American Review* 31:4; 567-578, Winter 1997.

In this article Harrison asserts that the Black Theater is experiencing an identity crisis. The Black Theater's unique cultural expression has been subdued because of the passive response of Blacks to the dominant culture which has subordinated Afrocentric culture. The Black Theater needs to define its ideological purpose and performance practice, Harrison argues.

376.   Morales, Donald M. "Do Black Theater Institutions Translate into Great Drama?" *African American Review* 31:41; 633-638, Winter 1997.

If African American drama is going to flourish, there must be African American institutions to support it. Morales discusses, historically, African American theatrical organizations which have and continue to exist in the United States.

377.   National Black Theater Festival, 1997. (Speech by August Wilson) (Transcript). *Callaloo* 20: 3; 483-493, Summer 1997.

This is a transcript of the address which playwright August Wilson gave at the National Black Theater Festival, August 4, 1997 in Winston-Salem, North Carolina. Wilson stresses the importance of recognizing the participation of Blacks in American theater. He observes that Black history, Black life, Black music, Black intelligence and Black humanity are represented in the Black theater. Wilson cautions against assimilation, because the process will damage the cultural identity of Blacks.

378.   West, Ron. "Others, Adults, Censored: the Federal Theatre Project's 'Black Lysistrata' Cancellation," *Theater Survey* 37:2; 93-114, November 1996.

West reports on the banning of African American adaptation of Aristophanes "Lysistrata" which was produced by an African American unit of the Federal Theater Project in Seattle, Washington, in 1936. City authorities banned the production because it was "viewed as a violation of social, sexual and racial hierarchies."

SELECTED DISSERTATIONS

379.   Burdine, Warren Buster, Jr. "The Evolution of the Images of African-American Characters in the American Commercial Musical." Ph.D. dissertation, City University of New York,

This study traces the evolution of images of African American characters in commercial musicals from the first decade of the twentieth century, when the operettas of Williams and Walker were being performed, to the present day. Myths and stereotypes about African-Americans that are portrayed by African American characters in these musicals are examined to determine their origin.

380.   Caple, Horace B. "Black Playwrights of the Federal Theater Project During the Great Depression: A Critical Analysis of Selected Works, 1945." Ph.D. dissertation, The Union Institute, 1991.

This study critically analyzes two plays by Black playwrights and one play by a white playwright who were employed on the Federal Theater Project (FTP). Caple's analysis revealed that African American playwrights on the FTP were very aware of their African sensibilities and made use of the art of dual communications in their plays. White playwrights, it was discovered, demonstrated that they were able to adapt skillfully this Black style of writing.

381.   DeFrantz, Thomas Faburn. "'Revelations': The Choreographies of Alvin Ailey." Ph.D. dissertation, New York University, 1997.

For the last thirty years of his life, Alvin Ailey (1931-1989) created a body of dance works which shaped African American participation in modern dance. DeFrantz examines Alvin Ailey's choreography in an attempt to analyze his aesthetic and explore theories of African American performance in relationship to Ailey's work.

382.   Krasner, David. "Resistance, Parody, and Double Consciousness in African American Theater, 1895-1910." Ph.D. dissertation, Tufts University, 1996.

Krasner examines the African American theater which flourished between 1895 and 1910 looking closely at its: (1) resistance to racism; (2) the emergence of parody; and (3) use of "double consciousness." The goal of this study is to illustrate that the Black theater from 1895 to 1910 was much more dynamic than it has traditionally been represented.

383.   Redd, Tina. "The Struggle for Administrative and Artistic Control of the Federal Theater Negro Units." Ph.D. dissertation, University of Washington, 1996.

Redd discussed the struggle experienced by African American personnel on the Federal Theater Project Negro Units in their efforts to gain a measure of artistic and administrative control over the Units. This study is divided into two parts. Part I examines the relationship between the Federal Theater Project and its parent organizations: Federal One and the Works Progress Administration. Part II examines the relationship between the administrative hierarchy and the Negro Units' productions.

384.   Williams, Elsie Arrington. "Jackie Moms Mabley: African American Performer." Ph.D. dissertation, University of Maryland, College Park, 1992.

Jackie Moms Mabley was the first African American woman to emerge as a single act comedic performer. Using historiography methodology, Williams gathered and compiled data on Mabley's life and career. He discussed Mabley as a popular entertainer whose comedic lore and life reflected African American cultural roots.

385.   Williams, Judith Michelle. "Nineteenth Century Stage Images of Black Women." Ph.D. dissertation, Stanford University, 1997.

A few plays written and produced in the nineteenth century had Black women characters. However, the stereotypical characters which emerged were akin to "Topsy" in *Uncle Tom's Cabin*, "the tragic mulatto," or "Mammy." This study explores the images used to portray black women in plays produced in nineteenth century America.

386.   Willis, Cheryl M. "Tap Dance: Memories and Issues of African-American Women
       Who Performed Between 1930 and 1950." Ph.D. dissertation, Temple University,
       1991.

       In this study Willis identified African American women ryhthm tap dancers who
       lived or performed on the East coast from the 1930s to the 1950s. Using oral
       interviews and related literature, Willis focused on the lives of these women rhythm
       tap dancers as entertainers, their contribution to the dance form, and their aesthetics
       of tap dance.

Singing, Hymning, Souling and Rapping: Blacks in Music

SELECTED REFERENCE WORKS

387.   Caldwell, Hansonia. *African American Music - A Chronology, 1619-1995.* Los Angeles: Ikora Communications, 1995.

This work presents an overview of African American accomplishments in music. It is a chronological record of developments in African American music from 1619 to 1995 with all musical genres represented. Included are an extensive bibliography as well as artist/recording and general indexes.

388.   Gray, John, comp. *Blacks in Classical Music: A Bibliographic Guide to Composers, Performers and Ensembles.* New York: Greenwood Press, 1985.

This is a comprehensive bibliography of books, parts of books, journal articles, and unpublished dissertations on Blacks who have been active as performers or writers of western or western-derived art music. Chapters are devoted to: (1) general works; (2) composers; (3) symphony and concert artists; (4) concert and opera singers; and (5) reference works and research centers. This work can be accessed through an artist index and an author index.

389.   Handy, D. Antoinette. *Black Conductors.* Metuchen, NJ: Scarecrow Press, 1995.

Containing profiles on more than 100 Black conductors and ensemble leaders, living and deceased, this is an useful reference source. Its main section has extensive profiles on 50 conductors. In a second section there are less substantive profiles on 50 additional conductors and ensemble leaders. Arranged alphabetically by surname in both sections, most profiles are accompanied with a photograph of the conductor or ensemble leader.

390.   Herzhaft, G'erard. *Encyclopedia of the Blues.* Translated by Brigitte Debord. Featuring the photography of Paul Harris, Jerry Haussler, and Anton J. Mikofsky. Fayetteville, AR: University of Arkansas Press, 1997.

Covering the years from 1920 to the present, this ready reference work presents information on musicians, trends, movements, geographical regions and producers of the blues. All entries are arranged alphabetically. The appendices include: (1) a bibliography; (2) a selected discography; (3) a list of blues anthologies on records; and (4) a list of the best blues standards.

391.   Horne, Aaron, comp. *Keyboard Music of Black Composers: A Bibliography.* Foreword by T. J. Anderson. Westport, CT: Greenwood Press, 1997.

This source contains works by Black composers of keyboard music who are living or lived on four continents: Africa, North America, South America, and Europe. Entries for composers are grouped under the continent where they lived or are living. Within each continent entries for composers are arranged alphabetically by surname. Each entry has the following items:(1) name of the composer; (2) birth date and, if appropriate, death date; (3) brief profile; (4) list of works composed; (5) bibliographic sources for additional information on the composer. A keyboard music index is included as well as an extensive discography and bibliography.

392.   Horne, Aaron, comp. *String Music of Black Composers: A Bibliography.* Westport, CT: Greenwood Press, 1991.

This source contains works by Black composers of string music who are living or lived on four continents: Africa, North America, South America, and Europe. Entries for composers are grouped under the continent where they lived or are living. Within each continent entries for composers are arranged alphabetically by surname. Each entry has the following items: (1) name of composer; (2) birth date and, if appropriate, death date; (3) brief profile; (4) list of works composed; (5) bibliographic sources for additional information on the composer. A performing medium index is included as well as an extensive discography and bibliography.

393.   Horne, Aaron, comp. *Woodwind Music of Black Composers.* Westport, CT: Greenwood Press, 1990.

This source contains 400 works by 100 Black composers of woodwind music who are living or lived on four continents: Africa, North America, South America, and Europe. Entries for composers are grouped under the continent where lived or are living. Within each continent entries for composers are arranged alphabetically by surname. Each entry has the following items: (1) name of composer; (2) birth date and, if appropriate, death date; (3) brief profile; (4) list of works composed; (5) bibliographic sources for additional information on the composer. A performing medium index is included as well as an extensive discography and bibliography.

394.   McCalla, James. *Jazz, A Listener's Guide.* 2nd, ed. Englewood Cliffs, NJ: Prentice-Hall, 1994.

Intended as a textbook for college students taking an elementary course in jazz or persons who have little or no knowledge of the subject, the goal of this work is to guide the student's listening of jazz. Technical terms are used which identify what elements to listen for in jazz composition. An anthology, *The Smithsonian*

Collection of Jazz, is recommended to be used with this aid.

395. Roach, Hildred. *Black American Music: Past and Present.* 2nd. ed. Malabar, FL: Krieger Publishing Co., 1994.

This work is an authoritative chronological survey of the development of African American music from the slave era to the 1990s. It is divided into three sections covering specific historical periods: "The Beginnings (1619-1870s)"; "The Awakening (1880s-1950s)"; "Freedom Now (1950-1990s)." A fourth section is entitled "The Pan-African Axis-Restoration and Reviviscence." The three appendices which enhance the reference value of this work are "Musical Terms and Selected Words"; "Readings, Recordings & Related Sources"; and "List of Composers, Publishers, Record Companies and Research Centers." A general index provides excellent access to this work by name, title and subject.

396. Sheridan, Chris, comp.   *Count Basie: A Bio-Discography.*   Westport, CT: Greenwood Press, 1986.

Count Basie recorded between 1929 and 1984. Some one thousand of Basie's recording sessions are arranged in this compilation in chronological order. For each session the following items are listed: location, musicians, tunes, duration, soloists, record label and number.

397. Smith, Eric Ledell. *Blacks in Opera: An Encyclopedia of People and Companies, 1873-1993.* Jefferson, NC: McFarland, 1995.

Information is presented in this work on over 500 Black composers, conductors, singers, dancers, choral directors, choreographers, critics, lighting designers and impresarios who were in opera between 1873 and 1993 as well as opera companies which employed Blacks during this period. Entries are arranged alphabetically by surname for persons and by official name for opera companies. Typical entries for persons include the following items: (1) name; (2) date of birth and, if appropriate, death date; (3) musical training; (4) repertoire; (5) name of opera companies or orchestras where artist performed; (6) recordings; (7) reviews; (8) bibliographic sources on the artist. Entries on opera companies include the following items: (1) name; (2) dates of existence; (3) executive officers; (4) locale of company; (5) repertoire; (6) featured performers. A general index provides access to the main body of the work.

398. White, Evelyn D. *Choral Music by Afro-American Composers: A Selected Annotated Bibliography. 2nd ed.* Lanham, MD: Scarecrow, 1996.

Originally published in 1981, the second edition of this work has been expanded to include over 1,000 compositions by 102 Afro-American composers and arrangers, living and deceased. Entries are arranged alphabetically by surname of the composer or arranger. Within the entry the following information is provided for each choral work cited: (1) title; (2) copyright date (first copyright date only); (3) number of pages; (4) vocal and solo requirements; (5) vocal range (s); (6) range of difficulty; (7) a cappella, type of accompaniment; (8) publisher; (9) catalog number, if available.

A title index to the bibliography provides references to composer or arranger. The following appendices are provided: (1) "Selected Collection of Negro spirituals"; (2) "Selected Discography"; (3) "Biographical Sketches of Composers and Arrangers"; and (5) "A Bibliography."

SELECTED TREATISES AND COMMENTARIES

Music, General

399.   Floyd, Samuel A., Jr., ed. *Black Music in the Harlem Renaissance: A Collection of Essays.* Knoxville: University of Tennessee Press, 1990.

The cultural climate created by the Harlem Renaissance not only promoted literature, as most commentators emphasize, but also supported the development of music and such musicians as William Grant Still, W. C. Handy, Duke Ellington, Eubie Blake and Fletcher Henderson. This collection of ten essays focuses on various aspects of Black music during the Harlem Renaissance. Among some of the essays included are "Vocal Concert Music in the Harlem Renaissance,"by Rawn Spearman; "Black Musical Theater and the Harlem Renaissance," by John Graziano; and "The Renaissance Education of Duke Ellington," by Mark Tucker.

400.   Floyd, Samuel A., Jr. *The Power of Black Music: Interpreting Its History from Africa to the United States.* New York: Oxford University Press, 1995.

In this highly theoretical study, Floyd traces the development of African American music from its African origins to the present. Floyd progresses from the assumption that African musical traits not only survived in African American culture, but played and continues to play a major role in shaping all forms of African American music.

401.   Jackson, Irene V., ed. *More Than Dancing: Essays on Afro-American Music and Musicians.* Westport, CT: Greenwood Press, 1985.

This collection of eleven essays, a project of the Center for Ethnic Music at Howard University, focuses on music and musicians in Africa and the Africa diaspora from an ethnomusicology perspective. Among some of the essays included are Portia K. Maulstby's "West African Influence and Retentions in US Black Music: A Sociocultural Study;" Horace Clarence Boyer's "A Comparative Analysis of Traditional and Contemporary Gospel Music;" and George L. Starks "'Salt and Pepper in Your Shoe': Afro-American Song Tradition on the South Carolina Sea Islands." 401

402.   Merlis, Bob and Seay, David. *Heart & Soul: A Celebration of Black Music Style in America, 1930-1975.* New York: Stewart, Tabori and Chang, 1997.

This is an illustrated history of African American popular music covering the years from 1930 to 1975. Using color reproductions of record labels as illustrations the authors focus their commentary on gospel, soul, R & B and jazz music recordings.

403.   Morgan, Thomas L. and Barlow, William. *From Cakewalks to Concert Halls: An Illustrated History of African American Popular Music from 1895 to 1930.*

Washington, DC: Elliot and Clark Publishing, 1992.

Covering the years 1895 to 1930, this is an illustrated history of popular African American music featuring spirituals, jazz, ragtime, and the blues. Included in this work are substantial profiles of such musicians and composers as J. Rosamond Johnson, James Weldon Johnson, William Marion Cook, Bert Williams and George Walker, James Reese Europe, Shelton Brooks, Joe Jordan, Noble Sissle and Eubie Blake, Cecil Mack, W. C. Handy, and Clarence Williams.

404.   Sacks, Howard. L. and Sacks, Judith R. *Way Up North in Dixie: A Black Family's Claim to the Confederate Anthem.* Washington, DC: Smithsonian Institution Press, 1996.

Daniel Decatur Emmett (1815-1904), a pioneer in American blackface minstrelsy, is generally credited with composing the Confederate anthem "Dixie Land." However, on the common gravestone of Ben and Lew Snowden, two Black musicians who knew Emmett, there is the following inscription: They Taught "Dixie" to Dan Emmett. In this intriguing treatise researchers Jack and Judith R. Sacks explore the claim that "Dixie Land" originated with Black musicians.

405.   Silverman, Jerry. *Just Listen to This Song I'm Singing: African-American History Through Song.* Brookfield, CT: The Millbrook Press, 1996.

Slave Songs of the United States, by William Frances Allen, Charles Pickard Ware, and Lucy McKim Garrison, which appeared in 1867, was the first attempt to publish and preserve the beauty of African American songs in the United States. Between 1867 and 1960 many African American songs have been published which reflect the spirit of the African American community during specific periods in history. Interpretative commentaries on 13 of these songs are presented in this illustrated volume. The songs are "Michael, Row the Boat Ashore"; "Go Down, Moses"; "Follow the Drinking Gourd"; "John Henry"; "Joe Turner"; "Casey Jones"; "The Ragtime Dance Song"; "Yellow Dog Blues"; "The Long-Line Skinner Blues"; "The Midnight Special"; "Don't You Leave Me Here"; "The Darktown Strutters' Ball"; and "We Shall Overcome."

406.   Southern, Eileen. *The Music of Black Americans: A History.* 3rd. edition. New York: Norton, 1997.

This classic work continues to be one of the most authoritative and comprehensive sources on the history of the development of African American music from 1619 to the present. In this third edition the coverage of women composers and performers has been expanded. A new chapter has been added entitled "Currents in Contemporary Arenas" and all appendices have been updated and expanded.

Sacred Music

407.   Allen, Ray. *Singing in the Spirit: African American Sacred Quartets in New York City.* Philadelphia: University of Pennsylvania Press, 1991.

This ethnographic study traces the stylistics of African American quartet singing in New York City from the 1920s to the 1980s. Allen spotlights the *a cappella* quartets of the 1920s, the shouting gospel quartets of the 1950s and the smooth contemporary quartets of the 1980s. This study is based on field recordings and interviews with many local New York City singers.

408.   Boyer, Horace Clarence. *How Sweet the Sound: The Golden Age of Gospel.* Photography by Lloyd Yeardwood. Washington, DC: Elliot & Clark, 1995.

This authoritative history of gospel music by one of the country's leading gospel scholars is divided into four chronological periods. They are "African American Sacred Folk Music: 1755-1945"; "Move On Up a Little Higher: 1945-1955"; "And the Walls Came Tumbling Down: 1955-1965"; and "Conclusion: I Look Down the Line and I Wondered: 1965 and Beyond."

409.   Harris, Michael W. *The Rise of Gospel Blues: The Music of Thomas Andrew Dorsey in the Urban Church.* New York: Oxford University Press, 1992.

The impact of gospel music on Black religion and culture has received only cursory attention by scholars. In this brilliantly conceived study Michael Harris considers the intellectual roots of gospel music in the person and career of Thomas A. Dorsey, the acknowledged "father" of the early gospel movement. As a composer, choir director and performer Dorsey and others launched the movement from Chicago in the late 1920s and early 1930s.

410.   Heilbut, Anthony. *The Gospel Sound: Good News and Bad Times.* Updated and revised, 5th Limelight Edition. New York: Limelight Editions, 1997.

A comprehensive survey of gospel music performers, this work has appeared in five editions since 1971. This fifth edition has an updated postscript which discusses developments in gospel music between 1986 and 1996.

411.   Jones, Arthur C. *Wade in the Water: The Wisdom of the Spirituals.* Maryknoll, NY: Orbis Books, 1993.

Jones, a musician-psychologist, interprets the meaning of six spirituals in six illuminating commentaries. The spirituals are: (1) "Over My Head I Hear Music in the Air"; (2) "Sometimes I Feel Like a Motherless Child"; (3) "Joshua Fit the Battle of Jericho"; (4) "City Call Heaven"; (5) "Scandalize' My Name"; and (6) "There Is a Balm in Gilead."

412.   Kirk-Duggan, Cheryl A. *Exorcizing Evil: A Womanist Perspective on the Spirituals.* Maryknoll, NY: Orbis Books, 1997.

Womanist theologian Kirk-Duggan, an ordained minister in the Christian Methodist Episcopal Church, discusses the history and meaning of spirituals from the womanist perspective. She focuses on the cultural forces which shaped their power for transformation. A trained musician, Kirk-Duggan, includes in her research methodology an analysis of taped live performances of spirituals done during the Civil Rights Movement when spirituals, as she observes, "spoke universally to the African-American community and promoted non-violence."

413. Lornell, Kip. *Happy in the Service of the Lord: African-American Sacred Vocal Harmony Quartets in Memphis.* 2nd edition. Knoxville: University of Tennessee Press, 1995.

Originally published in 1988 under the title *Happy in the Service of the Lord,* this second edition expands the examination of the development of African-American gospel quartets in Memphis, going ten years beyond the first edition. Covering the years from the 1920s to the mid-1990s, this second edition has a new section entitled "Selected Gospel Quartet Audiography," which lists some of the best recordings by regional and national African-American gospel quartets.

414. Reagon, Bernice Johnson, ed. *We'll Understand It Better By and By: Pioneering African American Gospel Composers.* Washington, DC: Smithsonian Institution Press, 1992.

The Smithsonian Institution's Program of Black American Culture conducted a study on the development of gospel music. Headed initially by the late Pearl Williams-Jones and ultimately by Bernice Johnson-Reagon, the fruits of the study, which involved gospel performers and informants, were presented in a series of conferences. This volume   includes papers which were given at the conferences by gospel music scholars on the works and lives of six pioneer gospel composers. The composers are Charles Albert Tindley, Lucie Eddie Campbell Williams, Thomas A. Dorsey, William Herbert Brewster, Sr. , Roberta Martin, and Kenneth Morris. A discography and annotated bibliography on gospel music are included.

415. Spencer, Jon Michael. *Black Hymnody: A Hymnological History of the African American Church.* Knoxville: University of Tennessee, 1992.

The hymnological tradition of the Black church is documented in this study. Spencer analyzes the hymnbooks of ten denominations representing Afro-Christians to determine shifts and developments in each denomination's theological and doctrinal tenets and social perspectives. Hymnals from the following denominations are analyzed: The African Methodist Episcopal Church; The African Methodist Episcopal Zion Church; The Christian Methodist Episcopal Church; The United Methodist Church; The National Baptists; The Church of God in Christ (Holiness), USA; The House of God Church; The Episcopal Church; and The Roman Catholic Church.

Secular Music

416. Carruth, Hayden. *Sitting In: Selected Writings on Jazz, Blues and Related Topics. Expanded edition.* Iowa City: University of Iowa Press, 1993.

This is a collection of essays, poems and reviews celebrating jazz and the blues. In these writings a sensitive poet/musician Carruth pays tribute to the African American's musical gift to America in such poems as "Joe Turner," "Song about Earl Hines," and such essays as "The Blues as Poetry" and "The Main Thing About Improvisation."

417.   Collis, John. *The Blues: Roots and Inspiration*. London: Salamander Books Limited, 1997.

With exceptional photographs and clear prose, this work charts the development of the blues from its roots in the South in the last decades of the nineteenth century through the 1970s. Profiles of many of the legendary blues artists are dispersed throughout the text, thus enhancing the reference of this work.

418.   Finn, Julio. *The Bluesmen: The Musical Heritage of Black Men and Women in the Americas*. New York: Interlink Publishing, 1992.

In the conclusion of this fascinating study, Finn observes: "the first slaves were the first blues people: America, literally, gave the first slaves the blues." This study surveys the development of the Blues from its origins in the slaves who were forcefully brought to Haiti, Jamaica, Cuba, Brazil, and the United States to the rise of the Black church in the nineteenth and early twentieth century to the 1990s.

419.   Hennessey, Thomas J. *From Jazz to Swing: African-American Jazz Musicians and Their Music, 1890-1935*. Detroit: Wayne State University Press, 1994.

Hennessey traces the development of jazz from its beginnings in New Orleans in the 1890s to 1935, the beginning of the Swing Era. This study notes the demographic, social, industrial, and political changes which were occurring during these years and discusses the profound influence they had on the development of jazz.

420.   Spencer, Jon Michael. *Blues and Evil*. Knoxville: University of Tennessee Press, 1993.

Several white scholars as well as some African Americans have viewed the Blues as evil or "the devil's music." Spencer argues that this viewpoint stems from a lack of knowledge or misunderstanding of African American culture. This study posits and develops the thesis that Blues are a reflection of the African American's religious cosmology.

421.   Trynka, Paul. *Portrait of the Blues*. Foreword by John Lee Hooker. Photographs by Val Wilmer. New York: Da Capo Press, 1997.

What are the roots of the Blues? What are Urban Blues? How are Blues played by different Blues musicians? How has Blues influenced other popular musical forms like Rock n' Roll and Be-Bop? In this work these and other questions are answered in the reported interviews with sixty Blues musicians. These African American musicians were, at the time of the interview, living in Blues rural and urban centers in the South and the North. Photographs by Val Wilmer witnessed the reported interviews and presents honest, unfiltered images of the interviewees and their physical surroundings. Brief biographies of the sixty interviewees are included in an appendix.

422.   Wheaton, Jack. *All That Jazz*. New York: Ardsley House, 1994.

This work is basically a textbook designed for college students enrolled in elementary courses in jazz appreciation or the adult layman with a non-musical background. Part I presents some facts about the history of jazz. Part II attempts to train an individual's jazz listening skills. Part III discusses the aesthetics, technological advances and social changes in the development of jazz.

Selected Biographical Works

423.   *The B. B. King Companion: Five Decades of Commentary*. Edited by Richard Kostelanetz; Assistant Editor Anson John Pope. New York: Schirmer Books, 1997.

During five decades of performing the Blues B. B. has frequently been heralded as the Master Bluesman. His exciting guitar playing and powerful vocals have thrilled millions. This unique collection of interviews of B. B. King and articles about the musician provide a comprehensive assessment of his life and musicianship.

424.   Badger, R. Reid. *A Life in Ragtime: A Biography of James Reese Europe*. New York: Oxford University Press, 1995.

In the years prior to World War I, James Reese Europe was one of the most influential orchestra leaders and musicians in the United States. His orchestra was the first African American music organization to perform in Carnegie Hall presenting "Symphony of the Negro" in 1912. During World War I, when his career was reaching its peak, Lt. Europe led the 369th Regiment's renown "Hellfighters Band." Badger has written a well-documented biography of this outstanding African American musician beginning with his birth in Mobile, Alabama, in 1880 and ending with his tragic and untimely death at the hands of one of his orchestra members on May 19, 1919 in Boston.

425.   Chilton, John. *Let the Good Times Roll: The Story of Louis Jordan and His Music*. Ann Arbor: University of Michigan Press, 1994.

Saxophonist and bandleader Louis Jordan was a perfectionist. Born in Brinkley, Arkansas, in 1908, Louis was the son of a musician, James Aaron Jordan, who decided early that Louis would follow in his footsteps. John Chilton's well-written biographical narrative tells the story of Louis Jordan's life highlighting the successful years of his popular band, "Louis Jordan and the Tympany Five."

426.   De Wilde, Laurent. *Monk*. Translated by Jonathan Dickinson. New York: Marlow & Company, 1997.

Although Theolonius Monk was born in Rocky Mount, North Carolina 1917, he considered himself a New Yorker, because he moved to the San Juan Hill District in Manhattan when he was four years old. De Wilde, a Frenchman, has written a biography which tracks the life of the jazz pianist-composer genius from his childhood years through the 1930s, 1950s and 1960s, when Monk was a struggling jazz artist seeking recognition, and through the 1970s, spotlighting his famous concert at Carnegie Hall in 1974, and through his years of madness in the late 1970s and finally to his death in 1982.

427.   Dixon, Willie. *I Am the Blues: The Willie Dixon Story.* New York: Da Capo Press, 1989.

Willie Dixon has made numerous contributions to Blues and Rock n' Roll as a songwriter, performer, producer and arranger. Among the musicians who have performed his songs and arrangements are Muddy Waters, The Doors, Chuck Berry, and The Rolling Stones. In this autobiography, written before his death in 1992, Willie Dixon recounts his life story from his birth in Vicksburg, Mississippi, where he was born in 1915, to his adult years in Chicago where he blossomed into an outstanding Blues musician.

428.   Gourse, Leslie. *Unforgettable: The Life and Mystique of Nat "King" Cole.* New York: St. Martin's Press, 1992.

Son of the Reverend Edward James Coles, Sr., Nathaniel Adams Coles, later known as Nat "King" Cole, was born in Montgomery, Alabama, in 1916. When Nat was four years old, his family moved to Chicago. Gourse relates these and other important events as she chronicles the life of Nat "King" Cole in this well-researched biography.

429.   Hajder, David. *Lush Life: A Biography of Billy Strayhorn.* New York: Farrar, Straus, Giroux, 1996.

There are many myths about Billy Strayhorn, who served as Duke Ellington's arranger for three decades. Some believe that Strayhorn had talent but little experience until Duke Ellington groomed him. Others assert that Strayhorn devoted his life to Ellington and did nothing outside the "Ellington orbit." David Hajder explodes these and other myths about Strayhorn in this biography by documenting his life from his birth in 1915 in Pittsburgh to his untimely death of cancer in 1967, focusing on the years from 1938 to 1967 when Strayhorn was a composer-arranger for Duke Ellington.

430.   Hasse, John Edward. *Beyond Category: The Life and Genius of Duke Ellington.* Foreword by Wynton Marsalis. New York: Da Capo Press, 1995.

In 1985 John Hasse, then a new curator at the Smithsonian Institution, held open talks with Mercer Ellington, Duke Ellington's son, to acquire the massive body of material which he had preserved on his father's life and career. Three years later this material was deposited in the Smithsonian Institution and Hasse begin to mine this new material on Ellington for this biography. Unlike most biographies on Ellington, which focus on his recordings, this is a "career" biography which documents Ellington's evolution as a musician and composer and looks at other facets of his life related to orchestra personnel, engagements, management style, economics, race, repertoire and creative style.

431.   Lester, James. *Too Marvelous for Words: The Life and Genius of Art Tatum.* New York: Oxford University Press, 1994.

Pianist Art Tatum's performing was notable for his touch, speed, accuracy, and harmonic and rhythmic imagination. Tatum was regarded as "a musician's musician" by many of his contemporaries. In this biography Lester attempts to focus on Tatum as a person as well as a musician. To gather information on Art Tatum, Lester interviewed over a hundred fellow musicians and friends. Portions of many interviews are included in the biography.

432.   Litweiler, John. *Ornette Coleman: A Harmolodic Life.* New York: Da Capo Press, 1994.

In the "Prologue" to this biography Litweiler asserts that Ornette Coleman with Buddy Bolden, Louis Armstrong and Charlie Parker are four artists whose music and presence were major turning points in jazz history. This biography of Coleman begins with his childhood in Fort Worth, where he was born in 1930, and continues through teen-age and young adult years. Litweiler concentrates on Coleman's adult years when he triumphed as a musician.

433.   Morton, David.C. *DeFord Bailey: Black Star of Early Country Music.* With Charles K. Wolfe. Knoxville: University of Tennessee Press, 1991.

African American DeFord Bailey, known as the "Harmonica Wizard," was the first musician to perform on the Grand Ole Opry radio station. During the 1920s and 1930s DeFord Bailey thrilled thousands when he performed at the Grand Ole Opry. Based on many hours of interviews with DeFord Bailey and his many friends at the Grand Ole Opry and the examination of archival materials on the Grand Ole Opry, this biography describes DeFord Bailey's life from his birth in 1899 in Smith County, Tennessee, to his death in Nashville in 1983.

434.   Nicholson, Stuart. *Billie Holiday.* Boston: Northeastern University Press, 1995.

Billie Holiday, a musical icon of twentieth-century music in America, greatly influenced contemporary vernacular singing. Between Billie Holiday's death in 1959 and 1995, six biographies have appeared on the artist. Nicholson, in his introduction to this new biography, indicates that he examined the aforementioned six biographies and found many flaws in each of them. This biography, according to Nicholson, has been meticulously researched. Nicholson's research methodology included: (1) a review of relevant archival material in numerous repositories; (2) a host of interviews with Billie Holiday's contemporaries; and (3) exploratory interviews with professionals who work in drug rehabilitation to acquire a greater understanding of Billie Holiday's drug addiction and treatment.

435.   Nisenson, Eric. *John Coltrane and His Quest.* New York: St. Martin's Press, 1993.

Although this book contains the important facts about Coltrane's life, Nisenson claims that it is not a formal biography. It is a work, according to Nisenson, which attempts, primarily, to explore the ideas and passions behind Coltrane's music.

436.   Robinson, Smokey. *Smokey: Inside My Life.* With David Ritz. New York: McGraw-Hill, 1989.

Since the early 1960s Bill "Smokey" Robinson has thrilled millions who have listened to his records and CDs. In this autobiography, Robinson, who is a gifted storyteller, candidly relates the story of his life from his childhood years in Detroit, where he was born in 1940, to the present, focusing on his years as a successful entertaining musician.

437.   Rogers, William Forrest. *Dorothy Maynor and the Harlem School of the Arts:The Diva and a Dream.* Lewiston, NY: E. Mellen Press, 1993.

In 1939 soprano Dorothy Maynor made her Town Hall debut to rave reviews, thus launching her career as a concert artist. For the next twenty-four years Dorothy Maynor presented concerts in the United States and abroad as well as made a host of recordings. After marrying and settling in New York City in 1963, Dorothy Maynor established the Harlem School for the Arts which has positively influenced the lives of many youths in Harlem. This biography recounts the life of Dorothy Maynor from her birth in 1910 in Norfolk, Virginia, to her stellar days on the concert stage and her years at the helm of the Harlem school for the arts.

438.   Simone, Nina. *I Put a Spell on You: The Autobiography of Nina Simone.* New York: Da Capo Press, 1993.

In person and on recordings Nina Simone has fascinated millions as a vocalist-pianist. Eunice Kathleen Wayman nee Nina Simone chronicles her life in this autobiographical narrative from her youth in Tryon City, North Carolina, where she was born in 1933, to her successful years as a entertainer-musician.

439.   Story, Rosalyn M. *And So I Sing: African American Divas of Opera and Concert.* New York: Warner Books, 1990.

Since the mid-nineteenth century African American divas have appeared in opera and on the concert stage in Europe, firstly, and the United States. Unfortunately, most of these African American divas have been ignored or overlooked by music historians. This collective biography attempts to fill this gap in American music history by presenting profiles of African American divas who performed in opera or on the concert stage from 1850 to the present.

440.   VIBE Magazine Editors. *Tupac Shakur, 1971-1996.* New York: Crown Publishers, Inc., 1997.

This illustrated biography of Tupac Shakur consists of a collection of essays and articles on various episodes in the short life of the talented hip hop musician. Included in the appendices is a time line of Shakur's life, a discography, and a filmography.

441.   Ward-Royster, Willa. *How I Got Over: Clara Ward and the World-Famous Ward Singers.* As told to Toni Rose. Foreword by Horace Clarence Boyer. Philadelphia: Temple University Press, 1997.

In 1931 Gertrude Murphy Ward and her two daughters, Clara and Willa, started a female gospel singing group. By 1970 the Ward Singers had become world renowned. This is the story of the hardships, frustrations and successes of this celebrated female gospel singing group.

442.   Wolff, Daniel. *You Send Me: The Life and Times of Sam Cooke.* New York: Quill, 1995.

Sam Cooke's recording "You Send Me" went to the top of the charts in 1957 and launched Cooke on a highly successful, but short-lived, career. Seven years later on a December night in 1964 Sam Cooke was found dead from a gunshot wound in a Los Angeles motel room. Wolff's biography documents Sam Cooke's young, fast-pace life from his youth in Cleveland, where he was born in 1931, to that fatal night in December 1964.

SELECTED PERIODICAL ARTICLES

443.   Bennighof, James. "Some Ramblings on Robert Johnson's Mind: A Critical Analysis and Aesthetic Value in Delta Blues," *American Music* 15:2; 137-295, Summer 1997.

Robert Johnson was a popular Delta blues singer and guitarist in the 1920s and 1930s,' who many Blues historians regard as a genius. Johnson had the ability to create a unique and singular musical statement within his style of music. Bennighof critically analyzes a single performance of Johnson's: his first take of "Rambling on My Mind" which was recorded in San Antonio on November 23, 1936.

444.   "The Birth of the Blues," *The Economist* 333:7964; 87-89, May 4, 1996.

The Blues influenced the development of all forms of music in the twentieth century. This article discusses the nature of this influence on jazz, rock 'n' roll, and other forms of popular music.

445.   Hardy, James Earl. "Hip Days in Gospel," *American Visions* 106:6;46-49, Dec. - Jan., 1995.

Since its inception gospel music has changed with each generation. Hardy discusses the historic evolution of the gospel sound from Thomas Andrew Dorsey, "The Father of Modern Gospel Music," in the 1930s to such contemporary gospel artists as Kirk Franklin, BeBe Winans, and Bobby Jones.

446.   "Is Gospel and R & B (Rhythm and Blues) Merging?" *Jet* 91:20; 62-66, April 7, 1997.

Contemporary gospel music has grown in popularity and has crossed over into the mainstream. But is contemporary gospel the result of gospel merging with rhythm and blues? In this article several gospel artists respond to this question in reported interviews. Among the gospel artists interviewed are Frank Hammond and Donnie McClurkin.

447.   Jackson, Joyce Marie. "The Changing Nature of Gospel Music: A Southern Case Study," *African American Review* 29:2; 185-191, Summer 1995.

Gospel music has evolved since the beginning of the twentieth century into a major component of the Black church. Jackson argues that the changing nature of gospel music can only be explained by examining all of the factors involved in the making of gospel music. The cultural, societal, and historical forces must be considered. In this case study Jackson analyzes the evolution of gospel music in New Orleans.

448.   Jones, Lisa C. "Are Whites Taking Gospel Music?" *Ebony* 50:9;30-43, July 1995.

In Spring 1995, when Angelo Torres, an Italian, nabbed the top Dove Award for the best Contemporary Black Gospel Recorded Song, many people were shocked. In this article Jones reports on the reactions of several Black gospel singers and composers to Torres's award and to the observation that white gospel singers like Carman, Amy Grant and the Petruccis are taking over gospel music.

449.   Komura, Edward. "Blues in the Round," *Black Music Research Journal* 17:1; 3-37, Spring 1997.

In this article Komura interprets and reports on Blues musician Eddie "Son" House's recollection of a 1930 recording session he had at Paramount Records with Charles Patron and two other Delta Blues musicians. All of the songs recorded are discussed and a discography of the session is included.

450.   Long, Worth. "The Wisdom of the Blues - Defining Blues as the True Facts of Life: An Interview with Willie Dixon," *African American Review* 29:2; 207-213, Summer 1995.

Willie Dixon (1912-1992) a Blues musician, composer, arranger and producer shares in this interview his insights into the performance of the Blues and gospel music. Dixon, who was influential in the development of the Blues, was labeled "the Poet Laureate of the Blues." This was probably Dixons last interview before he died in Chicago on January 29, 1992.

451.   Oulette, Dan. "'Hi, I'm the Boogie Man.'" *Down Beat* 64:6; 20-26, June 1997.

Oulette's interview with eighty year-old Blues musician John Lee Hooker answers many questions about the Blues icon. When did Hooker begin playing the Blues?

How does he define the Blues? What was his musical life like in Memphis during the 1940s? How did he feel the first time one of his records sold over a million copies? Who are his favorite Blues artists today?

SELECTED DISSERTATIONS

452.   Brown, Anthony L. "The Development of Modern Jazz Drumset Performance." Ph.D. dissertation, University of California, Berkeley, 1997.

Brown has developed an ethnomusicological study that focuses on the development of modern jazz drumming in the 1940s. Through transcription and critical analysis of recorded performances, Brown examines the stylistic innovations of African American drummers Max Roach, Kenny Clark and others. A historical survey of African American drumming traditions with a focus on jazz drumming is included.

453.   Hester, Karlton Edward. "The Melodic and Polyrhythmic Development of John Coltrane's Spontaneous Composition in a Racist Society." Ph.D., City University of New York, 1990.

An absorption of African and Asiatic music was central to Coltrane's musical evolution. In his musical development Coltrane systematically used the elements of five American musical styles: Blues, Bebop, Hardbop, "Modal Jazz," and his own "Free Jazz." His saxophone technique expanded the musical language for the saxophone as well as for all twentieth century performers. The intent of this study is to show the ways in which he achieved these accomplishments.

454.   Kohl, Paul Robert. "Who Stole the Soul? Rock and Roll, Race and Rebellion." Ph.D. dissertation. The University of Utah, 1994.

Kohl analyzes the reactions of several African American Blues and Jazz musicians on the impact and popularity of Rock and Roll music, which is based on African American-created Rhythm and Blues music. Among some of the African American musicians who were interviewed for this study were James Brown and Marvin Gaye.

455.   Lyle-Smith, Eva Diane. "Nathaniel Clark Smith (1877-1934): African American Musician, Music Educator, and Composer." Ph.D. dissertation, University of North Texas, 1993.

Nathaniel Clark Smith was one of the leading African American musicians, music educators and composers in the early decades of the twentieth century. This is a biographical study of his life and career. Smith published over fifty musical compositions. He taught music at Tuskegee University, Western University, Lincoln University (Mo.), Wendell Phillips High School (Chicago), and Sumner High School (St. Louis). Among some of his students who became prominent musicians were Charlie Parker, Lionel Hampton and Nat "King" Cole.

456.   McMichael, Robert Kenneth. "Consuming Jazz: Black Music and Whiteness." Ph.D. dissertation, Brown University, 1996.

Jazz as an art form originated in African American culture, McMichael observes. In this study McMichael views Jazz as a vehicle for social and cultural interaction between African Americans and whites. He examines relationships between performing African American jazz artists and white audiences.

457.   Parrish, Jon Seebart. "The Color of Jazz: Race and Representation in American Culture, 1945-1966." Ph.D. dissertation, University of California, Irvine, 1995.

During the twenty years following World War II, jazz was a nexus of interaction between African Americans and whites. This study seeks to show differences in the uses of jazz by African Americans and whites by comparing representations of Charlie Parker and other jazz performances in works by such white and African American writings as Jack Kerouac, John 'Clellan Holmes, Ross Russell, James Baldwin, John A. Williams, and William Melvin Kelley.

458.   Porter, Eric C. "'Out of the Blue': Black Creative Musicians and the Challenge of Jazz, 1940-1995." Ph.D. dissertation, University of Michigan, 1997.

This study is an intellectual history of African American jazz musicians covering the years 1940 to 1995. The primary sources which Porter used to develop this intellectual history are recordings, interviews with jazz musicians, liner notes, autobiographical material on jazz musicians, and significant writing by jazz musicians.

459.   Strong, Willie Frank. "Philosophies of African American Music History." Ph.D. dissertation, University of California, Los Angeles, 1994.

African American music, Strong observes, mirrors the political, social and political "currents" of the African community during any given historical period. This study examines the relationship between African American music and three "currents" from the late nineteenth century to the present. The three currents are nationalism, cultural aesthetics and musical historicism.

460.   Williams, Frank Douglas. "Rap Music in Society." Ph.D. dissertation, University of Florida, 1995.

Rap music is defined in this study as a late linguistic form of African American oral culture. Williams endeavors to : (1) explain rap's language; (2) give an in-depth perspective on the emergence of rap music in our society; (3) discuss ensuing lawsuits and efforts to censor rap musicians; and (4) describe rap music's impact on the mass media market.

Critiquing the Black Muse: Black Literary Criticism

SELECTED REFERENCE WORKS

461.   Bassett, John Earl. *Harlem in Review: Critical Reactions to Black American Writers, 1917-1939.* Selinsgrove, NJ: Susquehanna University Press, 1992.

Citations of critical reviews of works published by African American authors between 1917 and 1944 are presented in this work, which is divided into five chapters covering specific periods between 1917 and 1939 and an appendix for the years from 1940 to 1944. Within each chapter titles are arranged chronologically by date of first publication preceded by the phrase "Reviews of ...." Under each title citations to reviews are listed alphabetically by author of the review with a rating and a brief summary of the review. An "Index to Authors" and an "Index to Critics" provide access to the entire work.

462.   *Black Literature Criticism: Excerpts from Criticism of the Most Significant Works of Black Authors Over the Past 200 Years.* James P. Draper, editor. Detroit: Gale Research Inc. 1992.

This three-volume reference source presents excerpts of critical reviews of works published over the last two hundred years by 125 Black authors from the United States, Nigeria, Jamaica and more than a dozen other countries. Entries, which are arranged alphabetically by author with a photograph or illustration, include: (1) an informative biographical sketch of the author, focusing on their writing career; (2) listing of principle works published; (3) substantial excerpts of critical reviews with citations of works by the author.

463.   Chapman, Dorothy Hilton, comp. *Index to Poetry by Black American Women.* New York: Greenwood Press, 1986.

This work indexes 120 volumes of poetry authored by African American women and 83 anthologies of poetry containing poems by African American women. More than 4,000 poems by African American poets who published between 1746 and the present are included. Chapman developed three indexes to the work: "Title and First Line Index"; "Author Index"; and "Subject Index."

464.   Fabre, Michel J., et al., compilers. *The French Critical Reception of African-American Literature From the Beginnings to 1970: An Annotated Bibliography.* Westport, CT: Greenwood Press, 1995.

Michel Fabre, a brilliant authority on African American literature who has authored a definitive biography on Richard Wright and teaches at the University of Paris, has compiled this extensive bibliography of critical articles and essays on African American writers, many of whom lived in France, which appeared in French publications between 1900 and 1970. Many of the informative notations were written by Fabre.

465.   Foster, M. Marie Booth, comp. *Southern Black Creative Writers.* New York: Greenwood Press, 1988.

This is a bio-bibliography of Southern African American writers who: (1) lived in the former Confederate states, Maryland, Washington, DC, Kentucky and West Virginia; and (2) published literary works between 1829 and 1953. Entries are arranged alphabetically by author and include: (1) name; (2) birth and, if appropriate, death dates; (3) city and state of residency; (4) occupation; (5) bibliography of works published; (6) education; (7) other artistic and/or creative endeavors. Appendices in this work are: (1) authors grouped by states; (2) authors listed under four historical periods in which they were active.

466.   Jordan, Casper LeRoy. *A Bibliographical Guide to African American Woman Writers.* New York: Greenwood Publishing Group, 1993.

Citations of literary works published by African American women writers from 1746 to 1991 are presented in this reference guide. In the main body of this work, which covers the years 1740 to 1988 inclusively, entries are arranged alphabetically and numerically by author. Under each author's entry, primary sources are listed numerically followed numerically by secondary sources. Other sections of this work include: (1) a list of anthologies containing the works of African American women writers; (2) a list of general works; and "Supplement: Additional Writers and Sources, 1988-1991."

467.   *Masterpieces of African American Literature.* Edited by Frank N. Magill. New York: HarperCollins Publishers, 1992.

Critical essays on 149 literary works of universal appeal by African American writers from the poetry of Phillis Wheatley (ca 1770) to the novels of Alice Walker (1990s) are presented in this source. The genres included are novels, slave narratives, autobiographies, essays, short stories, and plays. Essays are signed and arranged alphabetically by the title of the literary work. An author and title index give excellent access to the entire work.

468.   Newby, James E. *Black Authors: A Selected Annotated Bibliography.* New York: Garland Publishing, Inc., 1990.

This comprehensive annotated bibliography has more than 3,000 entries to significant works authored, co-authored or edited by African Americans from 1773 to 1990. Entries are arranged by numerical sequence in nine chapters categorized by subject or genre. There are title and author indexes.

469.   *The Oxford Companion to African American Literature.* Editors: William Andrews; Frances Foster; and Trudier Harris. New York: Oxford University Press, 1997.

This well-researched, comprehensive one-volume work authoritatively documents more than 200 years of the African American literary tradition. Entries which are arranged in dictionary fashion consist of signéd essays on: (1) more than 400 African American writers, editors, and critics; (2) 150 major literary works; (3) hundreds of African American "icons" and literary characters; (4) major literary movements and terms; (5) African American publications and publishing; (6) African American literary genres; and (7) topics related to African American literature.

470.   *The Schomburg Guide to Black Literature: From the Eighteenth Century to the Present.* Roger M. Valade III, editor, with Denise Kasinec. Detroit: Gale Research Inc., 1996.

Utilizing the vast resources of the New York Public Library's Schomburg Center for Research in Black Culture, this comprehensive one-volume ready-reference is a compendium of information on Black literature and culture. Among its features are (1) bio-bibliographical essays on more than 500 authors, critics and literary personalities; (2) synopses of 400 major works; (3) essays on major African American literary themes, movements, genres, and terms; and (4) a chronology of major event in African American literary history.

SELECTED CONFERENCE

471.   *Afro-American Literary Study in the 1990s.* Edited by Houston A. Baker, Jr. and Patricia Redmond. Chicago: University of Chicago Press, 1989.

In April 1987 a conference was convened at the University of Pennsylvania entitled "The Study of Afro-American Literature: An Agenda for the 1990s." These proceedings present the seven major papers presented at the Conference. They are: "Canon - Formation, Literary History, and the Afro-American Tradition, From the Seen to the Told," by Henry Louis Gates, Jr.; "'Boundaries': Or Distant Relations and Close Kin," by Deborah E. McDowell; "Toward a Poetics of Afro-American Autobiography," by William L. Andrews; "The First-Person in Afro-American Autobiography," by Richard Yarborough; "There Is No More Beautiful Way: Theory and Poetics of Afro-American Women's Writing," by Houston A. Baker, Jr.; "Performing Blackness: Re/Placing Afro-American Poetry," by Kimberly W. Benston.

SELECTED TREATISES AND COMMENTARIES

472.   Andrews, William L., ed. *African American Autobiography: A Collection of Critical Essays.* Englewood Cliffs, NJ: Prentice-Hall,1992.

Theoretically, much of the new criticism of African American biography focuses on culturally specific analysis of works. This collection of thirteen essays reflects this new critical approach to analyzing African American biography. Among some of the essays included are "James Gronniosaw and the Trope of the Talking A book," by Henry Louis Gates, Jr.; *Crusader for Justice: Ida B. Wells,* by Joanne M. Braxton; and "Malcolm X and the Limits of Autobiography," by Paul John Eakin.

473.   Baker, Houston A., Jr. *Afro-American Poetics: Revisions of Harlem and Black Poetics.* Madison: University of Wisconsin Press, 1988.

In this reassessment of the Harlem Renaissance literature, Baker challenges cultural historians who have labelled the writings of such Harlem Renaissance writers as Countee Cullen, Claude Mckay and Nella Larsen as "provincial." Baker argues that the works of these writers were illustrative of "modernism."

474.   Carby, Hazel N. *Reconstructing Womanhood: The Emergence of the African American Woman Novelist.* New York: Oxford University Press, 1987.

Carby focuses on the development of African American women novelists in the nineteenth and early twentieth centuries. The women novelists considered are Frances Watkins Harper, Pauline Hopkins, Anna J. Cooper, Jesse Fauset and Nella Larsen.

475.   Connor, Kimbaerly Rae. *Conversions and Visions in the Writings of African American Women.* Knoxville: University of Tennessee Press, 1994.

Connor discusses religious conversion as a way of realizing self-identity portrayed in the works of African American women authors. Some of the writings discussed are *Incidents in the Life of a Slave Girl*, by Harriet Jacobs (1861); *Narrative of Sojourner Truth*, by Sojourner Truth (1852); *Sula*, by Toni Morrison; and *Dust Tracks on a Road*, by Zora Neale Hurston (1942).

476.   Ernest, John. *Resistance and Reformation in the Nineteenth Century African-American Literature.* Jackson: University Press of Mississippi, 1995.

Ernest examines six works by nineteeth century African American activist writers which challenged the conscience of the nation over the slavery and the race issue. The Six works are William Wells Brown's *Clotel; or The President's Daughter: A Narrative of Slave Life in America* (1853); Harriet E. Wilson's *Our Nig; or Sketches from the Life of a Free Black* (1859); Harriet Jacobs' *Incidents in the Life of a Slave Girl* (1861); Martin R. Delaney's *Blake: or the Huts of America; A Tale of the*

Mississippi Valley, the Southern United States, and Cuba (1859); Frederick Douglass'
My Bondage and My Freedom (1855) and *Frederick: Life and Times of Frederick
Douglass* (1881); and Frances W. Harper's *Iola Leroy, or Shadows Uplifted* (1892).

477.   Foster, Frances Smith. *Written By Herself: Literary Production of African American
Women, 1746-1892.* Bloomington: Indiana University Press, 1993.

Foster's study of the writings of African American women during the last half of the
18th century and almost the entire 19th century is thorough and well-documented.
Some of the writers discussed are Ellen Terry, Phillis Wheatley, Harriet Jacobs,
Frances Harper, and Anna J. Cooper.

478.   Gates, Henry Louis, Jr. *The Signifying Monkey: A Theory of African American
Literary Criticism.* New York: Oxford University Press, 1989.

Based on the assumption that each literary tradition "contains in it an argument for
how it can be read," Gates examines the relation of the Black vernacular tradition
to the African American literary tradition in an attempt to identify a theory of literary
criticism. In this work, Gates indentifies and explains this new theory of African
American literary criticism.

479.   Harper, Donna. *Not So Simple: The Simple Stories by Langston Hughes.* Columbia:
University of Missouri Press, 1995.

Harper's study of Langston Hughes' short stories: (1) traces the evolution of the
character of Jesse B. Semple from the weekly columns of the *Chicago Defender* to
its publication in two books; (2) evaluates the character's use of language and humor;
and (3) interprets the stories as commentaries on social history.

480.   Jablon, Madelyn *Black Metafiction: Self-Consciousness in African American
Literature.* Iowa City: University of Iowa Press, 1997.

In this study Jablon surveys literary theories currently applied to African American
fiction. She identifies "inductive" theories as arising from the corpus and 'extrinsic'
theories as applied to the corpus.

481.   Jackson, Blyden. *History of African American Literature: Volume 1: The Long
Beginning, 1746-1895.* Baton Rouge: Louisiana State University Press, 1989.

This is a meticulously-researched history of African American literature by a
seasoned scholar and professor. Jackson divides this work into historical era: "The
Age of Apprenticeship," which spans the years from 1746 to the late 1820s;
"The Age of Abolitionists, I," which covers the years from the late 1820s to the
1850s; and "The Age of Abolitionists, II," surveying years from the mid-1850s to the
1890s. Throughout this chronicle the author provides incisive analysis of many
works as well as concise profiles of authors.

482.   Jones, Gayl. *Liberating Voices: Oral Tradition in African American Literature.* Cambridge: Harvard University Press, 1991.

Jones discusses the techniques derived from African American oral genres which African American writers have used in their poetry, short stories and novels. Among the authors whose works are analyzed are Paul Laurence Dunbar, Langston Hughes, Ralph Ellison and Toni Morrison.

483.   *Language and Literature in the African American Imagination.* Edited by Carol Aisha Blackshire-Belay. Westport, CT: Greenwood Press, 1992.

This collection of essays represent a broad range of thinking on the development of the African American imagination in literature. The fourteen essays address four topics: (1) "The Afrocentric Imagination: Theory and Imagination"; (2) "Language Realities: Studies in Modern Societies"; (3) "Literary Analysis: Style and Substance"; and (4) "Reflective Designs in Literary Works."

484.   Lee, Valerie. *Granny Midwives and Black Women Writers: Double-Dutch Readings.* New York: Routledge, 1996.

Granny Midwives have played many roles in African American folk culture. In addition to delivering babies, they have been herbalists, health healers, storytellers, voodoo practicioners, palm readers, and spiritual leaders. Several African American women writers have drawn on African American folk culture to create Granny Midwives in their literary works. Lee examines the lives of real-life Granny Midwives in tandem with their fictional counterparts in the works of Toni Morrision, Toni Cade Bambara and Alice Walker.

485.   *Literary Influence & African American Writers: Collection of Essays.* Edited by Tracy Mishken. New York: Garland Publishers, 1996.

Some African American writers have been influenced by white writers, while others have been influenced by African American writers. This collection of essays discusses, in the words of the editor, "the influence of white writers on black ones."

486.   Nielsen, Aldon L. *Black Chant: Languages of African American Post Modernism.* New York: Cambridge University Press, 1997.

Nielsen traces the development of modernism and postmodernism in African American poetry in the decades following World War II. This study centers on the poetry of such avant-garde groups as The Umbra Group, Free Lance Poets, and The Howard-Dasein Poets.

487.   O'Neale, Sondra A. *Jupiter Hammond and the Biblical Beginnings of African American Literature.* Metuchen, NJ: Scarcrow Press; [Philadelphia, American Theological Association] 1993.

Jupiter Hammond, O'Neale observes, was the first African American to publish a comprehensive statement on Black theology in the United States (1760). In this work O'Neale presents the texts of six works by Hammond. Each text is introduced by a critical commentary by O'Neale. The six texts are "An Evening Thought: Salvation by Christ, with Penitential Cries" (1760); "An Address to Miss Phillis Wheatley" (1788); "A Poem for Children with Thoughts on Death" (1782); "An Evening's Improvement" and "A Dialogue Entitled The Kind Master and Dutiful Servant" (n.d.); and "An Address to the Negroes in the State of New York." (1982).

488.   Wall, Cheryl. *Women of the Harlem Renaissance.* Bloomington: Indiana University Press, 1995.

Jesse Redmond Fauset, Nella Larsen and Zora Neale Hurston were the three major women writers of the Harlem Renaissance. In this study Cheryl Wall focuses on the lives of these three writers and critically discusses their works. The lives and achievements of other women writers and personalities who were active during the period are spotlighted by Wall such as Georgia Douglas Johnson, Marita Bonner, Gwendolyn Bennett and Bessie Smith.

489.   Wilentz, Gay Alden. *Binding Cultures: Black Women Writers in Africa and the Diaspora.* Bloomington: Indiana University Press, 1992.

This study explores the cultural bonds between African women writers and women writers of African descent in the diaspora. Wilentz discusses similiarities in the works of African American women writers Alice Walker, Toni Morrison and Paule Marshall and African women writers Flora Nwapa, Efua Sutherland and Ama Ata Acdoo.

490.   Wright, Lee Alfred. *Identity, Family and Folklore in African American Literature.* New York: Garland Publishers, 1995.

Wright examines the disintegration of the African American family portrayed in African American literature since the mid-nineteenth century. The novels included in this study are *Clotel*, by William Wells Brown (1853); *The Conjure Woman,* by Charles W. Chestnutt (1899); *Meridian*, by Alice Walker (1976); *The Color Purple*, by Alice Walker (1982); *The Bluest Eye*, by Toni Morrison (1970); *Sula*, by Toni Morrison (1973); *The Street*, by Ann Petry (1946); and *The Incidents in the Life of a Slave Girl*, by Harriet Jacobs (1861).

BIOGRAPHICAL WORKS

491.   *African American Writers.* Edited by Valerie Smith, Lea Baechler and A. Walton Litz. New York: Collier Books, 1993.

Critical biographies on twenty-eight African American writers who were active from 1820 to the early 1890s are presented in this collective biography. These writers include slave narrators, fiction writers, playwrights, poets and feminist writers.

492.   *Black American Poets and Dramatists Before the Harlem Renaissance.* Edited by Harold Bloom. New York: Chelsea House, 1994.

Biographical profiles and critical commentaries on the works of eleven African American writers who were active between 1760 and the 1940s are presented in this work. A chapter devoted to each writer includes the following information: (1) a biographical outline on the writer; (2) excerpts of critical commentaries on the writer's works; and (3) a listing of the writer's work citing title and date of publication. The following writers are included: William Stanley Braithwaite, William Wells Brown Joseph Seamon Cotter, Jr., Paul Laurence Dunbar, Jupiter Hammond, Francis E. W. Harper, George Moses Horton, Oscar Micheaux, Phillis Wheatley, Albery Allison Whitman.

493.   Davis, Thadious M. *Nella Larsen, Novelist of the Harlem Renaissance: A Women's Life Unveiled.* Baton Rouge: Louisiana State University Press, 1994.

Nella Larsen was found dead in her New York apartment on March 30, 1964. After 1940, this Harlem Renaissance writer, who authored the novels *Quicksand* (1928) and *Passing* (1929), seemed to have lost communication with her fellow writers and colleagues. Thadious M. Davis recreates the life of this elusive and mysterious African American woman writer chronicling her youthful years in her native Chicago, active years as a popular writer in the 1920 and 1930s, campus life at Fisk University where she was married to physicist Elmer Samuel Imes, and the years between 1940 and 1964 when she seemed to live a life of self-imposed loneliness.

494.   Fabre, Michael. *From Harlem to Paris: Black American Writers in France: 1840-1980.* Urbana: University of Illinois Press, 1991.

The experiences of African Americans who visited or lived in France between 1840 and 1980 are the subject of this study. To develop this study, Fabre interviewed several living African American writers. He also examined the correspondence of dead and living writers, as well as published and unpublished works.

495.   Gabbin, Joanne V. *Sterling A. Brown: Building a Black Aesthetic.* Westport, CT: Greenwood Press, 1985.

When *Southern Road,* Sterling A. Brown's first book of poetry, was published it was praised by James Weldon Johnson, Alain Locke, Louis Untemeyer and other literary commentators as an important work and launched Brown into the mainstream of American literature. During his long career as a poet, critic, and teacher, Brown has been a major influence on the development of African American and American literature. Joanne V. Gabbin has written a literary biography of Brown beginning with a discussion of the antecedent literary enviroment into which he was born in Washington, D. C. in 1901 and continuing throughout his life spotlighting influences and forces which shaped literary aesthetics.

496.   *Major Black American Writers Through the Harlem Renaissance.* Edited by Harold Bloom. New York: Chelsea House Publishers, 1995.

Substantive information on eleven African American writers is presented in this collective biography. A chapter is devoted to each writer containing the following information: (1) a biographical outline; (2) excerpts of critical writings on the author's works; and (3) a listing of published works by the author citing title and publication date. The authors included in this work are Charles W. Chestnutt, W. E. B. DuBois, Langston Hughes, Zora Neale Hurston, James Weldon Johnson, Claude Mckay, Jean Toomer, and Richard Wright.

497.   Tillery, Tyrne. *Claude McKay: A Black Poet's Struggle for Identity.* Amherst: University of Massachusetts Press, 1992.

Claude McKay, a Jamaican, who emigrated to the United States in 1912 to attend Tuskegee Institute, found his way to New York City by 1914, where he began his writing career after failling as a restaurant owner. In the years that followed, McKay, novelist and poet, became "the first Black writer to make the best-seller list" (*Home to Harlem, 1928).* Tillery's biography of McKay presents a psychological portrait of the complex writer and focuses on his problems with identity, vocation and politics.

SELECTED PERIODICAL ARTICLES

498.   Brown, Fahamisha Patricia. "And I Owe It All to Sterling Brown: The Theory and Practice of Black Literary Studies," *African American Review* 31:3; 449-454, Fall 1997.

Sterling A. Brown has been called "The Father of Black Literary Studies." Through his representations of Black characters in novels, motion pictures, television shows, Brown provided a vocabulary and methodology to the approach of Black Studies. This writer pays homage to Brown in this article. "His earliest work, the 1931 *Outline for the Study of the Poetry of American Negroes,* inspired me to produce an 'Outline for the Study of Poetry in the African World' in 1971, when I taught my first course in Black Poetry."

499.   Gates, Henry Louis, Jr. "Harlem On Our Minds," *Critical Inquiry* 24:1; 1-12, Autumn, 1997.

In the 1990s African Americans are, according to Gates, presently experiencing the fourth cultural renaissance in the twentieth century as evidence by the remarkable output of African Americans in contemporary literature, music, drama, dance, television, motion pictures and philosophy. Gates identifies three other periods in the twentieth century when African Americans experienced a cultural renaissance and compares these periods to the 1990s.

500.   George, Stephen K. "The Horror of Bigger Thomas: The Perception of Form Without Face in Richard Wright's *Native Son*," *African American Review* 31:3; 497-505.

Although Bigger Thomas is a product of adverse racial and social forces, which has been the subject of many studies, George seeks to discuss what these forces have done to Bigger's spirituality. How does Bigger perceive people? What is the quality of his personal relationships with his family and his girlfriend?

501.   McElrath, Joseph R., Jr. "W. D. Howells and Race: Charles W. Chestnutt Disappointment of the Dean," *Nineteenth Century Literature* 51:4; 474-500, March 1997.

From February 1900 to December 1901, novelist Charles W. Chestnutt enjoyed the favor of novelist-editor William Dean Howells, who encouraged the writing of Paul Laurence Dunbar and Booker T. Washington. However, Howell's negative review of Chestnutt's novel *The Marrow of Tradition* (1901) shocked the author. McElrath discusses Howell's review and possible reasons behind it and the Chestnutt reaction.

502.   Obejas, Achy. "In Profile: E. Lynn Harris," *The Advocate* 736:110-113, June 24, 1997.

E. Lynn Harris is the best-selling African American gay author in the United States today. This article profiles Harris focusing on his struggling years as a writer whose first book was self-published and self-distributed to African American bookstores. Today, Harris relates that his books are popular with gay as well as "straight" readers.

503.   Ramsey, Priscilla R. "John Edgar Wideman's First Fiction: Voice and the Modernist Narrative," *CLA Journal* 41:1; 1-23, September 1997.

Ramsey critically discusses Wideman's first three novels: *A Glance Away* (1967); *Hurry Home* (1970); and *The Lynchers* (1973). These novels reflect a modernist outlook which Ramsey argues is distinct from his later post-modern voice.

504.   Reid, Calvin. "Leon Forrest's Chicago," *Publishers Weekly* 244:48; 17-18, November 24, 1997.

Reid reports on the death of acclaimed Chicago writer Leon Forrest on November 7, 1997. Forrest, who was a professor at Northwestern University, was regarded as a writer of almost Joycean technique. Forrest leaves a legacy as a brilliant chronicler of African American life in Chicago. Much of Forrest's work is out of print. One novel, *Divine Days* (1993) and a collection of essays, *Relocation of the Spirit* (1994), are still in print. Henry Louis Gates, Jr. hailed *Divine Days* as the *War and Peace* of the African American novel.

505.   Roberts, Kimberly. "The Clothes Make the Woman: The Symbolics of Prostitution in Nella Larsen's *Quicksand* and Claude McKay's *Home to Harlem*," *Tulsa Studies in Women's Literature* 16:1; 107-131, Spring 1997.

Using prostitution as a metaphor, Roberts analyzes the dress of women in Nella Larsen's novel *Quicksand* and Claude McKay's novel *Home to Harlem* to determine the position of African American writers in the publishing industry. In both novels prostitutes dressed in exotic, color clothes which distinguished them from respectable middle-class women.

506.   Rowell, Charles H. "'Beyond the Hard Work and Discipline': An Interview with Leon Forrest," *Callaloo* 20:2; 342-357, Spring 1997.

In one of Leon Forrest's last interviews before his death on November 7, 1997, he talks about his craft. He tells us that he started writing as a poet and expanded his poetic language into writing a novel. "The most poetic of my novels would be the first one *There is a Tree More Ancient Than Eden* (1973) -- there I was trying to work with poetry in, really, the epic form." Throughout this interview Forrest answers many questions about his development as a writer. How does he feel about rewriting? What are his insecurities? How has the tradition of storytelling influenced his writing? How did he learn how to read texts of other authors critically? And what influence did Toni Morrison, as an editor and writer, have on him?

507.   Rowell, Charles H. "An Interview with Charles Johnson," *Callaloo* 20:3; 531-548, Summer, 1997.

Novelist and short story writer Charles Johnson was awarded the National Book Award for his third novel, *Middle Passage,* in 1990. Johnson reveals that he, a former cartoonist, has a passion for drawing. Contemporary African American literature, Johnson believes, lacks philosophical fiction.

508.   Rowell, Charles H. "An Interview with Clarence Major," *Callaloo* 20:3; 667-679, Summer 1997.

Clarence Major, who has authored volumes of poetry, novels and works of non-fiction, presents an absorbing interview. Major tells us that he is a visual thinker and draws on his experiences in painting when writing fiction.

509.   Tellery, Carolyn. "The Fiction of Black Crime: It's No Mystery," *AmericanVisions* 12:2; 18-22, April-May, 1997.

The landscape of mystery writers is changing. More African American mystery novelists are entering the publishing mainstream. Tillery pays homage to the "pathfinders" Chester Himes and Walter Moseley. She discusses the novels of African American mystery writers Nora Deborah, Barbara Neeley, Gar Anthony Haywood and Terris McMahan Grimes.

510.   Young, Mary E. "Anita Scott Coleman: A Neglected Harlem Renaissance Writer," *CLA Journal* 40:3; 271-284, March 1997.

Anita Scott Coleman was an essayist, short story writer, poet and screenwriter who began writing in the early years of the Harlem Renaissance and continued publishing through 1961, when a volume of her poetry, *The Singing Bells*, was published posthumously. Young discusses Coleman's short stories, essays and screen scenarios.

SELECTED DISSERTATIONS

511.   Asgill, Edmondson Omatayo. "The Endangered Species: The African Characters in American Fiction." Ph.D. dissertation, University of South Florida, 1988.

The differences in the characterization of Africans in the fictional works of Euro-American writers and African American writers is the subject of this study. Asgill observes that Euro-Americans, because of negative attitudes toward Africans, tend to create African characters that are caricatures and unrealistic. African American writers, because of racial pride coupled with their reaction to the caricatures of Africans in works by Euro-American writers, develop sentimentalized African American characters in their fictional works, which are just as unrealistic as the caricatures they observe in Euro-American writers.

512.   Auger, Philip George. "Rewriting Afro-American Manhood: Negotiations of Discursive Space in the Fiction of James Baldwin, Alice Walker, John Edgar Wideman and Ernest Gaines." Ph.D. dissertation, University of Rhode Island, 1995.

Augurs attempts to describe how four African American novelists "re-write" negative social narratives of Black manhood similar to that presented by Richard Wright in his development of Bigger Thomas in *Native Son* (1940). The treatment of negative social narratives of Black male protagonists in four novels are discussed: James Baldwin's *Giovanni's Room* (1956); John Edgar Wideman's *Philadelphia Fire* (1990); Alice Walker's *The Third Life of Grange Copeland* (1972); and Ernest Gaines' *A Lesson Before Dying* (1993).

513.   Barnes, Paula Cassandra. "Traditions and Innovation: Toni Morrison and the Flight Motif in Afro American Literature." Ph.D. dissertation, The University of Michigan, 1988.

The flight motif is a tradition in Afro American literature. It was used in Richard Wright's *Native Son* and Ralph Ellison's short story "Flying Home." Toni Morrison in *Song of Solomon* employs the flight motif using the same predominate themes and images found in the aforementioned works by Wright and Ellison. However, Morrison "examines, manipulates, revises or transforms these themes." Barnes discusses how Morrison innovates on the flight motif in *Song of Solomon* and the influence Morrison has had on other African American writers.

514.   Beavers, Herman, Jr. "Wrestling Angels Into Song: Coherence and Disclosure in the Fiction of Ernest J. Gaines." Ph.D. dissertation, Yale University, 1990.

Beavers explores the impact of Ralph Ellison's concept of aesthetics, as found in *Invisible Man*, on the fiction of Ernest J. Gaines and James Alan McPherson. Gaines' novel, *Of Love and Dust*, and McPherson's short story, "A Solo Song: For Doc" are analyzed to show the nature of Ellison's influence.

515.   Brown, Kenneth James. "The Lean Years: The Afro-American Novelist During the Depression." Ph.D. dissertation,.The University of Iowa, 1987.

Brown asserts that the period of the 1930s has been inaccurately described as the era in which Afro-American novelists only produced protest novels. In this study Brown attempts to refute this assessment by examining novels published by Afro-American novelists between 1929 and 1940. In his examination of these novels Brown classifies these novels thematically into three categories.

516.   Carroll, Michael Charles. "Music As Medium for Maturation in Three Afro-American Novels." Ph.D. dissertation, The University of Nebraska-Lincoln, 1991.

Music is a major force in African American life. Many writers have used music because of its improvisational nature and vernacular appeal. This study analyzes the use of music to catalyze the maturation of young male characters in three novels. The novels are *Go Tell It on the Mountain*, by James Baldwin (1953); *Snakes*, by Al Young (1970); and *Train Whistle Guitar*, by Albert Murray (1974).

517.   Pinson, Hermine Dolorez. "The Aesthetic Evolution of Melvin B. Tolson: A Thematic Study of His Poetry." Ph.D dissertation, Rice University.

Pinson views Melvin B. Tolson as an enigmatic figure in the context of Afro-American and Euro-American modernism. This study traces the development of aesthetics in the poetry of Tolson by analyzing all his poetry from his first manuscript, *Portraits in a Harlem Gallery*, which was published posthumously in 1979, to his last work, *Harlem Gallery: Book I, The Curator* (1965).

518.   Plant, Deborah G. "Zora Neal Hurston's *Dust Tracks on a Road*: Black Biography in a Different Voice." Ph.D. dissertation, University of Nebraska-Lincoln, 1988.

Zora Neale Hurston's autobiography *Dust Tracks on a Road* has been labelled by some critics as shallow, dishonest and disingenuous. This revisionist study re-examines this work. Plant lauds the work's stylistic merits, authenticity and profundity. She attributes its poor reception to a tradition in African American literature which favors the works by male writers.

519.   Zafar, Rafia Margaret. "White Call, Black Response: Adoption, Subversion, and Transformation in American Literature from the Colonial Era to the Age of Abolition." Ph.D. dissertation, Harvard University, 1989.

This study reassesses the literature produced by African American writers from the Colonial Era to the years of the abolition of slavery. Zafar examines the adaptation and transformation of literary forms by African American writers and compares them to parallel works of white writers in these literary forms. The comparison, Zafar argues, shows that African American writers were not just imitative but added their own innovations to the canon literary forms.

Author–Title Index

American Music, 443

American Philosophical Association, 043, 046

American Speech, 274

American Visions, 445, 509

"An Analysis of the African American Catholic Congregation as a Social Movement," 120

"An Analysis of the Conception of Love and Its Influence on Justice in the Thought of Martin Luther King, Jr.," 051

"Ancient Africa and the Old Testament," 083

"The Ancient Kemetic Roots of Library and Information Science," 129

"And I Owe It all to Sterling Brown: The Theory and Practice of Black Literary Studies," 498

And So I Sing: African American Divas of Opera and Concert, 439

Anderson, Monica, 257

Anderson, T. J., 391

Andrews, William L., 469, 471-472

Angelou, Maya, 314

"Anglo-American and Nigerian Jurisprudence: A Comparison and Contrast in Legal Reasoning and Concept of Law," 055

"Anita Scott Coleman: A Neglected Harlem Renaissance Writer," 510

Anthony, Jacqueline, 207

Appiah, Anthony, 028

Are Blacks Spiritually Inferior to Whites?, 087

"Are Whites Taking Gospel Music?" 448

Art Documentation: Bulletin of the Art Libraries Society of North America, 152

Art in America, 322

The Art of Archibald Motley, Jr., 313

The Art of Black Women: Works of Twenty-Four Artists of the Twentieth Century, 289

The Art of John Biggers: View from the Upper Room, 315

Arthur Alfonso Schomburg: Black Bibliophile and Collector: A

Biography, 145

Arts of Black Folk Conference for Community Organizations: Presenting Black Folk Arts, 217

Asgill, Edmondson Omatayo, 511

Ashe, Traditional Religion and Healing in Sub-Saharan Africa and the Diaspora: A Classified International Bibliography, 062

"The Atlantic Creoles and the Language of the Ex-Slave Recordings," 261

Attille, Martina, 312

Auger, Philip George, 512

Authority Control: Principles, Applications, and Instructions, 138

The B. B. King Companion: Five Decades of Commentary, 423

Bad Faith and Antiblack Racism, 023

Badar, Barbara, 146

Badger, R. Reid, 424

Baechler, Lea, 491

Bailey, David A., 312

Bailey, Guy, 261

Bailey, Randall, 083

Baker, Houston A., 471, 473

Ball, Patricia Bernice Huff, 158

Bambara, Toni Cade, 348

Banner, William Augustus, 017, 035

Barboza, Steven, 101

Barlow, William, 403

Barnell, Andrea D., 312

Barnes, Paula Cassandra, 513

Barney, Deborah Verdice Smith, 208

Baron, Robert, 217

Bascio, Patrick, 084

Bassett, John Earl, 461

Battle, Thomas C., 143

Baugh, John, 270

Bearden, Romare, 300

Bearing Witness:Contemporary Works by African American Women Artists, 314

Beavers, Herman, Jr., 514

"Becoming an Evil Society: The Self

"Marketing the Inner City Library,"
129
Marsalis, Wynton, 430
Marszalek, John F., 008
Martin, Robert Sidney, 153
Martinez, Roy, 044
"Mary Beattie Brody and the
Administration of the Harmon
Foundation," 311
"Master-Slave Dialectic in the
Writings of Ralph Ellison:Toward
a Neo-Hegelian Synthesis," 052
*Masterpieces of African American
Literature,* 467
Masthead, 205
Maultsby, Portia K., 401
Maxwell, Joe, 114
McCalla, James, 394
McCann, Donnarae E., 141, 161
McCloud, Aminah Beverly, 102
McDaniel, M. Akura, 314
McDonald, Isaac Lee, 125
McDonogh, Gary W., 096
McDowell, Deborah E., 471
McElrath, Joseph R., Jr., 501
McEvilley, Thomas, 322
McFarlane, Adrian, 020
McGregory, Jerrilyn M., 253
McMichael, Robert Kenneth, 456
McMillan, Terry, 348
McMillen, Liz, 273
McNeil, Jesse Jai, Sr., 076
McPheeters, Annie L., 136
Media Studies Journal, 202
Meisenhelder, Susan, 245
"The Melodic and Polyrhytmic
Development of John Coltrane's
Spontaneous Composition in a Racist
Society," 453
Melton, J. Gordon, 061
*Membership Directory of the Black
Caucus of the American Library
Association,* 128
"The Mental Property of the Nation," 311
Mercer, Valerie J., 323
Merlis, Bob, 402
"Metamorphosis: The Life and Art of
John Biggers," 315

Microform Review, 156
Mikofsky, Anton J., 390
*Miles of Smiles, Years of Struggle:
Stories of Black Pullman Porters,*
236
"The Million Man March," 050
Mills, Charles, 045
Mills, Emma Joyce White, 163
Minton, John, 226
Mishken, Tracy, 485
"The Missing Tradition," 322
Mitchell, Henry H., 073
"Modality in Jamaican Creole," 270
Modern Theology, 113
"Modern Tones, 312
Monk, 426
Montgomery, Michael, 261
Moody-Adams, Michele Marcia, 054
Moon, Spencer, 360
Moorhus, Donita, 189
"Moral Philosophy Naturalized:
Morality and Mitigated
Scepticism in Hume," 054
Morales, Donald M., 376
*More Than Dancing: Essays on
Afro- American Music and
Musicians,*401
Morgan, Thomas, 403
Morrison, Keith, 296
Morrison-Reed, Mark, 103
Mortimer, Owen, 371
Morton, David C., 433
Moses, Sibyl E., 154
"Motley's Chicago Context," 311
*"MOVE: News Coverage of
Confrontations, Philadelphia,
1978-1987: A Cultural Studies
Approach,"* 214
Mufwene, Salikoko S., 261, 267,
270, 274
Munir, Fareed Z., 126
"Multiple Modals 12 [2] 505 0 in
United States Black English:
Synchronic and Diachronic
Aspects," 270
Murphy, Larry G., 061
"Music As Medium for Maturation in
Three Afro-American Novels,"

516
The Music of Black Americans: A History, 406
Myers, Ardie S., 132
Myers, Willia H., 077, 078
Myhill, John, 270

"Nathaniel Clark Smith (1877-1934): African American Musician, Music Educator, and Composer," 455
National Black Theater Festival, 1997, 377
N'Diaye, Diana Baird, 217
*Necessary Questions: An Introduction to Philosophy,*028
"Neglected Resource of Scholarship," 242
Negro Almanac, 006
Nella Larsen, Novelist of the Harlem Renaissance: A Women's Life Unveiled, 493
Nelson, Timothy J., 115
New York Public Library, 133, 134
Newby, James E., 468
Newman, Mark, 187
Nichols, Nichelle, 363
Nichols, Patricia C., 270
Nicholson, Stuart, 434
Nielsen, Aldon L., 486
Nineteenth Century Literature, 501
"Nineteenth Century Stage Images of Black Women," 385
Nisenson, Eric, 435
Nitty Gritty: A White Editor in Black Journalism, 188
Nnam, Michael Nkuzi, 055
"Non-Cartesian Sums: Philosophy and the African American Experience," 045
Not So Simple: The Simple Stories by Langston Hughes, 479
*Notable Black American Women,*014
Notable Black American Women, II, 014
Null, Gary, 349

"Oakland Amends Ebonics Resolution," 275
Obejas, Achy, 502
O'Brien, Patrick Michael, 214
Ochs, Stephen, 097
Ogunleye, Tolagbe, 246

Okpara, Mzee Lasana, 031
Old Ship of Zion: The Afro-Baptist Ritual in the African Diaspora, 093
Oldfield, J. R., 107
On Race and Philosophy, 024
"On the Infinitive in Gullah," 270
"One Meaning of 'Mo' Better Blues,'" 348
O'Neale, Sondra A., 487
Onyewuenyi, Innocent Chilaka, 038
Oprah! Up Close and Down Home, 362
The Origin of Black English: "Be" Forms in Hoodoo Texts, 263
The Original African Heritage Bible: King James Version, 057
Ornette Coleman: A Harmolodic Life, 432
"Oscar Micheaux's Interrogation of Caricature as Entertainment," 374
"Others, Adults, Censored: The Federal Theater Project's 'Black Lysistrata,'" 378
Oulette, Dan, 451
" 'Out of the Blue': Black Creative Musicians and the Challenge of Jazz, 1940-1995," 458
Outlaw, Lucius T., 016, 024
"An Outline of an Economic Ethics for Developing Countries," 049
Owens, Reginald Lee, 215
The Oxford Companion to African American Literature, 469

P. B. Young, Newspaperman: Race Politics and Journalism in the New South, 1910-1962, 195
Pacific Division Conference, American Philosophical Association, 046
Paris, Peter J., 116
Parish, James, 356-357
Parker, David L., 132
Parrish, Jon Seebart, 457
"The Passive in Caribbean English Creole," 270
"The Past is Prologue But is Pastiche

Subject Index

"Home of the Brave" (Film), 340
Home to Harlem, 497, 505
hooks, bell, 341
Hoodoo doctors, 263
Hooker, John Lee, 451
Hopkins, Pauline, 474
Horton, George Moses, 492
House, Eddie "Son," 449
House of God Church, 415
Houston, Texas, 111, 162
Houston, Whitney, 356
The Howard-Dasein Poets, 486
Howard University, 143, 223, 401
Howells, William Dean, 501
Hughes, Langston, 009, 479, 482, 496
Hume, David, 054
Hunt, Richard, 292
Hunter, Clementine, 289, 310
Hunter-Gault, Charlayne, 190-191,
    194, 198
Hurry Home, 503
Hurston, Zora Neale, 072, 230, 240,
    245, 475, 488, 496, 518;
    Bibliography, 221
Hymns, 415

Identity, ethnic, 032
Identity, interracial, 027
Ideology, 029
Ifa, 053
Illinois, 178
Illustrators, 142
Images and stereotypes, 045, 147, 161,
    164, 181, 183, 343-344, 359, 361,
    364, 374, 379, 385
Imes, Elmer Samuel, 493
"In Dahomey" (Musical), 367
"In Living Color" (Television Program),
    359
"In the Heat of the Night" (Film), 353
Incidents in the Life of a Slave Girl,
    475-476, 490
Indexes, general, 004-005
Indiana, 178
Information superhighway, 130
Infant mortality, 215
Intellectuals, 025
The International Review of African

American Art, 325
Invisible Man, 052
Iola Leroy, or Shadows Uplifted, 476
Iowa, 178
Islam, *See* Muslims

Jackson Advocate (Mississippi), 196
Jackson, Janet, 356
Jackson-Jarvis, Martha, 296
Jacobs, Harriet, 232, 475-477, 490
Jamaica, 269-270, 418, 462, 497
Jameson, J. Franklin, 155
Jasper, John, 124
Jazz, 006, 223, 286, 394, 402-403,
    416, 419, 422, 426, 432, 444,
    452-453, 456-458
Jefferson, Thomas, 132
,Jemison, T. J., Sr., 105
Jet, 188
Jews and Judaism, 037, 098
Jews, Black , 098
"Joe Turner" (Song), 405
"John Henry" (Song), 405
Johnson, Charles, 507
Johnson-Cochran, Dwayne, 345
Johnson, Donn, 199
Johnson, Georgia Douglas, 488
Johnson, James Weldon, 072, 198,
    230, 495-496
Johnson, John H., 198
Johnson, Joshua, 292, 310
Johnson, Robert, 443
Johnson Publishing Company, 189
Johnson-Reagon, Bernice, 414
Johnson, Sargent, 312
Johnson, William H., 152, 303, 309-
    312, 331
Jonah's Gourd Vine, 230
Jones, Bobby, 445
Jones, Frank, 310
Jones, Lois Mailou, 289
Jones, William A., 069
Jordan, James Aaron, 425
Jordan, Joe, 403
Jordan, Louis, 425
Josephite Society of the Sacred Heart,
    097
Josey, E. J., 157

Petry, Ann, 490
Phelps-Stokes Fund, 154
Philadelphia, 214, 253, 282
Philadelphia Fire, 512
Philanthropic foundations, 153-155
Philosophy, 016-055; African, 053;
    Database, 016
Phinazee, Annette Lewis, 131
Photographers and photography, 293-
    294, 306, 308-309, 311; Bio-
    bibliography, 293-294
Pierce, Delilah, 289
Pindell, Howardina, 289, 297
"Pinky" (Film), 340
Pittsburgh, Pennsylvania, 159, 304, 429
Plato, 211
Plays, 337-338
Playwrights, 337-338, 364, 368, 373,
    491
Poets and poetry, 010, 139-140, 280,
    416, 463, 471, 486, 491-492, 495,
    498, 508, 510, 517
Poindexter, Delores "Sugar, 208
Poitier, Sidney, 353
"The Policy Players" (Musical), 367
Politics, 025, 029, 080, 156, 182, 207,
    209
Porter, Charles E., 310
Portraits in a Harlem Gallery, 517
Pot liquor, 238
Powell, Adam Clayton, 250
Preaching, 070-071 073-074, 076,
    124-125
Presidential debates, 1992, 193
Priests, African American, 097, 100
Producers (television), 201
Program of Black American Culture,
    Smithsonian Institution, 414
Prostitutes, 505
Protest, 067
Proverbs, 227
Psychologists, 022
Public libraries and librarianship, 129-
    130, 133-134, 136, 158-159,
    162-163
Publishers and publishing, 011, 129-
    130, 150, 157
Pulitzer Prize, 204, 373

Pullman porters, 236
Purdue University, 043

Quicksand, 493, 505
Quilting, 295, 307
Quincy, Illinois, 222

Racism, 023, 120
Radio, 179, 184-187, 193, 208, 337;
    Bibliography, 166
Ragtime, 403
"The Ragtime Dance Song" (Song), 405
Raleigh, North Carolina, 315
"Rambling on My Mind" (Song), 443
Randolph, A. Philip, 236
Rape, 215
Rapping and rap music, 246, 265, 277,
    281, 286, 440, 460
Reconstruction, 156
Reference works, 001-015
Reid, Tim, 345
Religion, 006, 036, 056-127, 156, 222;
    African, 062; Bibliography,
    059, 062; Biographical
    dictionary, 060; Directory, 058;
    Encyclopedia, 061
Religionwissenschaft School, 119
Republican Party, 209
Richardson, Willis, 368
Ringgold, Faith, 289, 324
Riots, 156
Roach, Max, 452
Roberts, Malika, 289
Robinson, Jackie, 358
Robinson, William "Smokey," 436
Rocky Mount, North Carolina, 426
The Rolling Stones, 427
Rome, Georgia, 136
Rose McClendon Players, 008
Rowan, Carl T., 192
Ruffin, Josephine St. Pierre, 194
Ruley, Ellis, 305
Rumors, 231
Rural communities, 249, 254
Russell, Ross, 457
Russwurm, John B., 198

Sacred music, 252, 407-415

About the Compiler

DONALD FRANKLIN JOYCE is Dean of Library and Media Services at Austin Peay State University. He is the author of *Gatekeepers of Black Culture: Black-Owned Book Publishing in the United States, 1817–1981* (Greenwood, 1983), *Blacks in the Humanities, 1750–1984: A Selected Annotated Bibliography* (Greenwood, 1986), and *Black Book Publishers in the United States: A Historical Dictionary of the Presses, 1817–1990* (Greenwood, 1991).

ISBN 0-313-30477-7

90000>

EAN

9 780313 304774

HARDCOVER BAR CODE